Editor
Eric Migliaccio

Editorial Project Manager
Ina Massler Levin, M.A.

Editor-in-Chief
Sharon Coan, M.S. Ed.

Illustrator
Howard Chaney

Cover Artist
Jessica Orlando

Art Coordinator
Denice Adorno

Imaging
Alfred Lau
James Edward Grace
Rosa C. See

Product Manager
Phil Garcia

Publishers
Rachelle Cracchiolo, M.S. Ed.
Mary Dupuy Smith, M.S. Ed.

Enhancing Writing
with Visuals

Grades 1-2

Written by

Jennifer Overend Prior, M.Ed.

Teacher Created Materials, Inc.
6421 Industry Way
Westminster, CA 92683
www.teachercreated.com
ISBN-1-57690-987-5

©2000 Teacher Created Materials, Inc.
Made in U.S.A.

Table of Contents

Introduction 3

Summary of Standards for Language Arts 4

Visuals for Reports 7

Report Cube—Research Poster—Research Wheel—Postcard Booklet—Paper Plate Mobile—Travel Brochures—Research Riddle Books—Using Maps to Enhance Reports—Cardinal Directions—Reading and Making Map Keys—Using World Maps—Using Weather Maps—Picture Diagrams—Venn Diagrams—Category Diagrams—Making Slideshow Presentations

Visual Aids for Journalism 34

Class Graphs—Reading Bar Graphs—Making Bar Graphs—Pictographs—Making Computer Graphs—Reading Tally Charts—Making Tally Charts—Surveys—Calendar Charts—Classroom Maps—Community Maps—Newsletters

Visuals for Book Reports 67

Story Events—Character Collage—Character Puzzles—Story Stew—Finger Puppets—Book Report Block—Story Setting—Story Picture Frame—Story Menus

Visuals for Narratives 79

Mysterious Shapes—What's in the Box?—I Was So Afraid—What Is That Fluffy Thing?—Something Is Under my Bed!—Under the Sea—Splat—Caught in the Web—Magic Glasses—Who Lives Here?—Poppin' Good Story—Pop-Up Book—Mini Book

Visuals for Topics 96

Riding in an Airplane—Icky Bugs, Cool Bugs—Recycled Robots—Living Plant House—Ocean Booklet—Holiday Greetings—Descriptive Rainbows—Shape Writing

More Visual-Aid Projects 120

Paints, Dough, and Techniques—Stencils—Class Scrapbooks—Individual Portfolios—Planning a Presentation

Assessment 131

Using Rubrics—Writing Mechanics Rubric—Content and Organization Rubric—Visual Aids (General) Rubric—Maps and Diagrams Rubric—Charts and Graphs Rubric—Skills Checklist—Writing and Visuals Self-Assessment

Answer Key 142

Bibliography 144

Introduction

Teaching children to write well is of great importance in today's classrooms. This resource will help to provide inspiration for your children that will motivate them to express themselves creatively through writing.

This book is divided into five main categories. Included are writing and visual-aid ideas for reports, journalism, book reports, narratives, and selected topics that may accompany units you already use in class. Some of the projects for the sections include the following:

- **reports**—projects such as research posters, research wheels, travel brochures, maps, diagrams, and multimedia presentations
- **journalism**—projects such as graphs, surveys, charts, classroom and community maps, and newsletters
- **book reports**—projects such as game boards, collages, puppets, dioramas, and book report blocks
- **narratives**—activities such as writing frames, pop-up books, and mini books
- **topics**—topics such as airplanes, bugs, robots, planting seeds, ocean animals, and greeting cards.

Each lesson begins with a teacher-directed activity, including prewriting activities, steps involved in the assignment, and publishing ideas. Many of the lessons include student activity pages for reinforcement of more difficult skills.

Through writing, your children will be able to perfect basic writing skills. By integrating these lessons into your language-arts program, your children will strengthen their skills while creating written work and visual projects that can be shared with and enjoyed by others.

The skills within each lesson are grade-level appropriate and linked to the Language Arts Standards. On pages 4–6, you'll find a list of the standards for kindergarten through second grade. At the top of each lesson, you'll find a reference to one or more of the standards. By using the lessons in this book, your children will be exposed to many of the skills needed in order to move toward mastery of the Language Arts Standards.

The assessment section of this book provides a variety of tools for evaluating student written work and visual projects. You'll find several rubrics appropriate for different types of writing assessment. You'll also find a self-assessment sheet for the children and a skills checklist for you to record mastery of the standards.

While using the lessons in this book, feel free to allow your children's creativity to flow; then, watch as the intriguing visual projects in this book enliven your children's writing in all subject areas.

Standards for Language Arts
Grades K–2

Accompanying the major activities of this book will be references to the basic standards and benchmarks for writing that will be met by successful performance of the activities. Each specific standard and benchmark will be referred to by the appropriate letter and number from the following collection. For example, a basic standard and benchmark identified as **1A** would be as follows:

Standard 1: Demonstrates competence in the general skills and strategies of the writing process

Benchmark A: Prewriting: Uses prewriting strategies to plan written work (e.g., discusses ideas with peers, draws pictures to generate ideas, writes key thoughts and questions, rehearses ideas, records reactions and observations)

A standard and benchmark identified as **4B** would be as follows:

Standard 4: Gathers and uses information for research purposes

Benchmark B: Uses books to gather information for research topics (e.g., uses table of contents, examines pictures and charts)

Clearly, some activities will address more than one standard. Moreover, since there is a rich supply of activities included in this book, some will overlap in the skills they address, and some, of course, will not address every single benchmark within a given standard. Therefore, when you see these standards referenced in the activities, refer to this section for complete descriptions.

Although virtually every state has published its own standards and every subject area maintains its own lists, there is surprising commonality among these various sources. For the purposes of this book, we have elected to use the collection of standards synthesized by John S. Kendall and Robert J. Marzano in their book *Content Knowledge: A Compendium of Standards and Benchmarks for K–12 Education* (Second Edition, 1997) as illustrative of what students at various grade levels should know and be able to do. The book is published jointly by McRel (Mid-continent Regional Educational Laboratory, Inc.) and ASCD (Association for Supervision and Curriculum Development). (Used by permission of McRel.)

Language Arts Standards

1. Demonstrates competence in the general skills and strategies of the writing process

2. Demonstrates competence in the stylistic and rhetorical aspects of writing

3. Uses grammatical and mechanical conventions in written compositions

4. Gathers and uses information for research purposes

Standards for Language Arts *(cont.)*
Grades K–2

1. Demonstrates competence in the general skills and strategies of the writing process

A. Prewriting: Uses prewriting strategies to plan written work (e.g., discusses ideas with peers, draws pictures to generate ideas, writes key thoughts and questions, rehearses ideas, records reactions and observations)

B. Drafting and Revising: Uses strategies to draft and revise written work (e.g., rereads; rearranges words, sentences, and paragraphs to improve or clarify meaning; varies sentence types; adds descriptive words and details; deletes extraneous information; incorporates suggestions from peers and teachers; sharpens the focus)

C. Editing and Publishing: Uses strategies to edit and publish written work (e.g., proofreads using a dictionary and other resources; edits for grammar, punctuation, capitalization, and spelling at a developmentally appropriate level; incorporates illustrations or photos; shares finished product)

D. Evaluates own and others' writing (e.g., asks questions and makes comments about writing, helps classmates apply grammatical and mechanical conventions)

E. Dictates or writes with a logical sequence of events (e.g., includes a beginning, middle, and ending)

F. Dictates or writes detailed descriptions of familiar persons, places, objects, or experiences

G. Writes in response to literature

H. Writes in a variety of formats (e.g., picture books, letters, stories, poems, and information pieces)

2. Demonstrates competence in the stylistic and rhetorical aspects of writing

A. Uses general, frequently used words to convey basic ideas

Standards for Language Arts *(cont.)*

Grades K–2

3. Uses grammatical and mechanical conventions in written compositions

A. Forms letters in print and spaces words and sentences

B. Uses complete sentences in written compositions

C. Uses declarative and interrogative sentences in written compositions

D. Uses nouns in written compositions (e.g., nouns for simple objects, family members, community workers, and categories)

E. Uses verbs in written compositions (e.g., verbs for a variety of situations, action words)

F. Uses adjectives in written compositions (e.g., uses descriptive words)

G. Uses adverbs in written compositions (i.e., uses words that answer how, when, where, and why questions)

H. Uses conventions of spelling in written compositions (e.g., spells high frequency, commonly misspelled words from appropriate grade-level list; uses a dictionary and other resources to spell words; spells own first and last name)

I. Uses conventions of capitalization in written compositions (e.g., first and last names, first word of a sentence)

J. Uses conventions of punctuation in written compositions (e.g., uses periods after declarative sentences, uses question marks after interrogative sentences, uses commas in a series)

4. Gathers and uses information for research purposes

A. Generates questions about topics of personal interest

B. Uses books to gather information for research topics (e.g., uses table of contents, examines pictures and charts)

Visuals for Reports

Report Cube

Research Poster

Research Wheel

Postcard Booklet

Paper Plate Mobile

Travel Brochures

Research Riddle Books

Using Maps to Enhance Reports

Cardinal Directions

Reading and Making Map Keys

Using World Maps

Using Weather Maps

Picture Diagrams

Venn Diagrams

Category Diagrams

Making Slideshow Presentations

Report Cube

After the children gather research information, have them create report cubes to creatively display a short report.

Materials

- one copy of the report cube pattern on page 9
- scissors
- pencil
- crayons or colored pencils
- glue

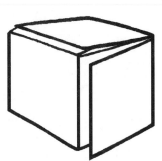

Directions

1. Cut out the report cube.
2. On sections one, two, four, and five, write sentences about the topic.
3. On sections three and six, draw pictures about your topic.
4. Assemble the cube, folding on the dotted lines and gluing on the tabs.

Standards and Benchmarks: 1A, 1B, 1C, 1H, 3B, 4A, 4B

Research Poster

A poster is a great way to display research information. Your children can create eye-catching posters with this project.

Materials

- copy of the poster planning sheet on page 10
- crayons, colored pencils, or markers
- posterboard or tagboard
- ruler or yardstick
- pencil

Directions

1. Use the poster planning sheet to plan the information and illustrations to be placed on the poster.
2. Create an enlarged version of the poster on posterboard or tagboard.
3. Use a ruler or a yardstick to create straight, centered lines for writing research information.
4. Use a pencil to write information and draw illustrations. This makes it easier to correct mistakes that might be made. Then use crayons, colored pencils, or markers to trace over the pencil lines.

Report Cube

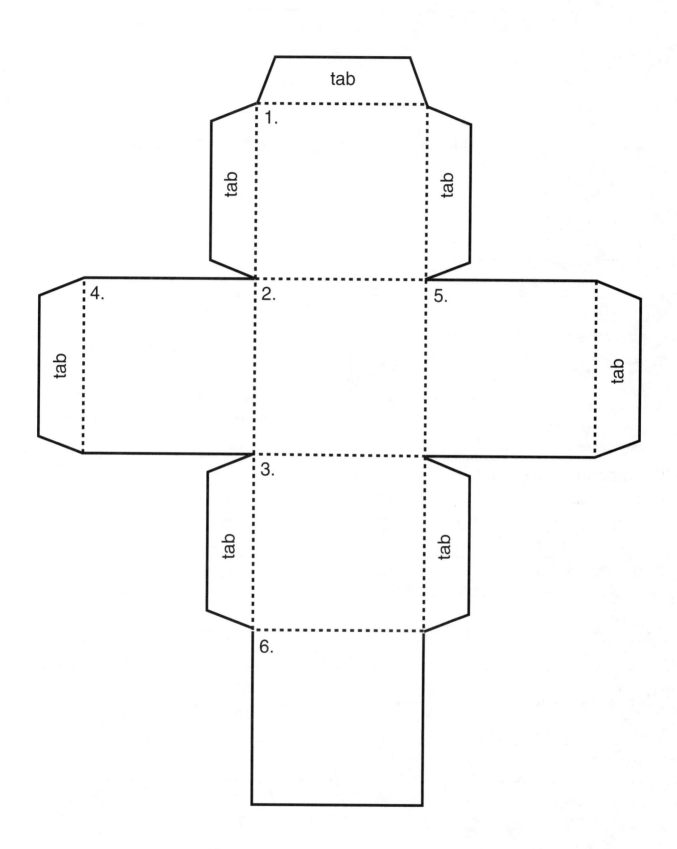

Poster Planning Sheet

_____

(title of the report)

Write about your topic.

_____

_____

_____   ┌─────────────────────────┐
                                      │   │
_____   │   │
                                      │   │
_____   │   │
                                      │   │
_____   │   │
                                      │   │
_____   │   Draw an illustration │
                                      │   of your topic.   │
_____   └─────────────────────────┘

Write about your illustration.

_____

_____

_____

_____

_____

Write about what you learned about the topic.

_____

_____

_____

_____

Research Wheel

There are many ways to present research reports. One creative way is the research wheel.

Materials

- copies of pages 12 and 13
- scissors
- pencil

- crayons or colored pencils
- brass fastener

Directions

1. Duplicate copies of pages 12 and 13 for each child.

2. Cut out the wheels on the bold lines as well as the dotted window on the illustration wheel.

3. Write portions of the report in the divided sections of the wheel on page 13.

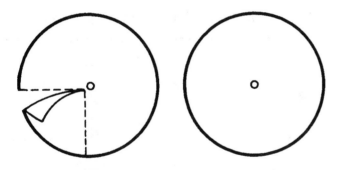
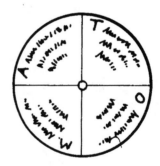

4. Create an illustration on the wheel on page 12.

5. To assemble the project, place the illustration wheel atop the report wheel. Press a brass fastener through the center dots.

6. The report wheel is read by turning the top wheel to reveal the information below.

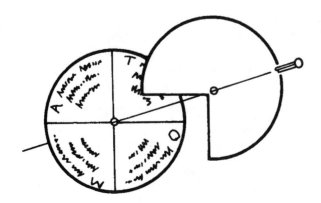
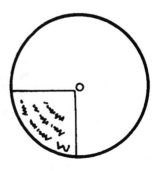

Research Wheel

Illustration Wheel

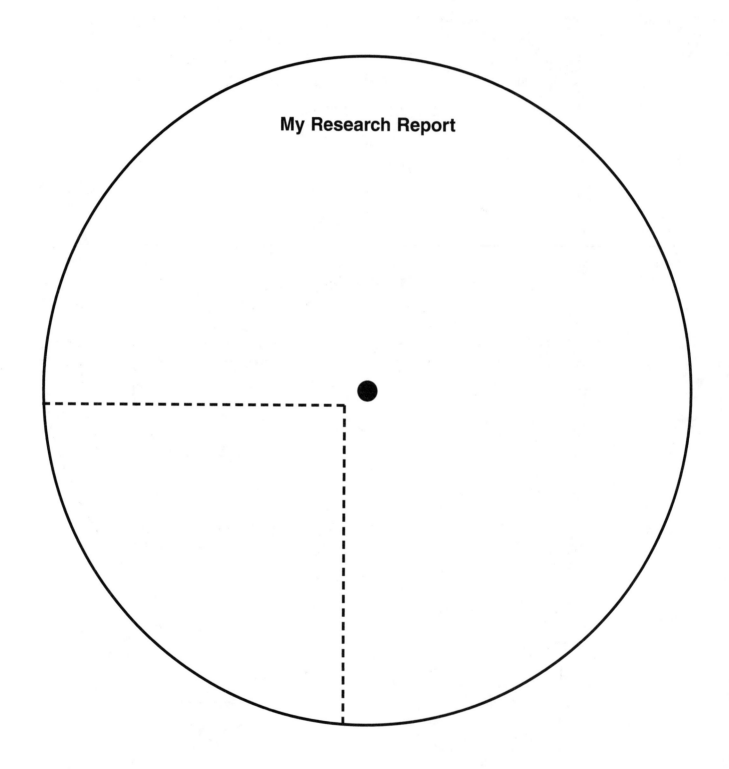

My Research Report

Research Wheel

Report Wheel

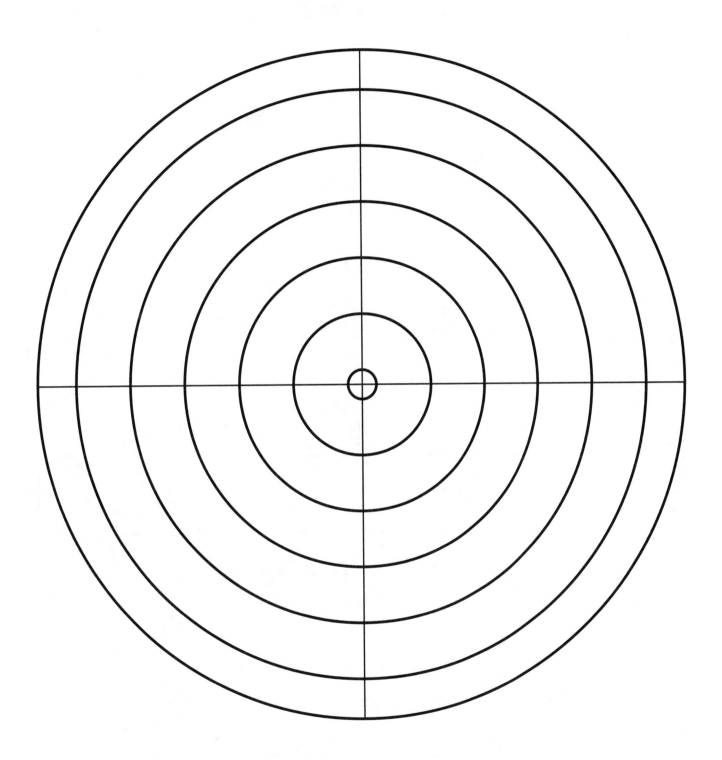

Postcard Booklet

A postcard booklet can be written to convey information about interesting locations in the country and throughout the world. To make a postcard booklet, follow the directions below.

Materials

- copies of the postcard templates on page 15
- scissors
- two 4" x 6" (10 cm x 15.2 cm) sheets of construction paper
- stapler
- pencil
- crayons or colored pencils

Directions

1. Cut out the desired number of postcard templates.
2. Stack the postcards with the blank sides facing up. Place a sheet of construction paper atop and below the stacked pages and staple the booklet together along the left edge.
3. Color a picture of a different location or object on the front of each postcard.
4. On the back of each, write a name and address, as well as a short letter telling about the location or object.
5. Decorate the cover and label it with the name of the booklet, such as "Great Vacation Spots," "Rainforests of the World," or "Animals of the Southwest."

Paper Plate Mobile

Your children can create informative mobiles with this easy-to-make project.

Materials

- 2 paper plates
- pencil
- hole puncher
- crayons or colored pencils
- glue
- length of yarn

Directions

1. In the center of each paper plate, color a picture about the topic.
2. Write two or three sentences about each picture.
3. Glue the backs of the plates together and allow the glue to dry.
4. Use a hole puncher to punch a hole in the top of both plates.
5. Tie the yarn through the holes.

Postcard Templates

To

_____

_____

_____

To

_____

_____

_____

Travel Brochures

Present research information by making a travel brochure.

Materials

- large sheet of light-colored construction paper
- crayons or colored pencils
- pencil

Directions

1. Fold the large sheet of construction paper horizontally in thirds (accordion-style or with two outside flaps folding inward). You now have six rectangular panels to work with.

2. On the front panel of your brochure, draw a picture about your topic. Use crayons or colored pencils to write the name of the topic or location.

3. Then add a slogan to capture attention, such as "Once you arrive, you'll never want to leave!" Write your name at the bottom of this panel.

4. Use the remaining panels to write portions of the report and make accompanying illustrations.

Research Riddle Books

This is a fun way for children to present their newfound research information.

Materials

- one sheet of 9" x 13" (22.8 cm x 32.9) construction paper
- crayons or markers
- scissors
- stapler

Directions

1. To assemble a booklet, fold the construction paper in half.

2. Next, fold the paper in half again, as shown.

3. Cut the top of the two shorter folded edges as shown.

4. Staple along the left edge to secure the booklet.

5. Decorate the cover and write a title relating to the topic.

6. Write a riddle relating to the topic on the front of each page with an answer on the back. See the example below.

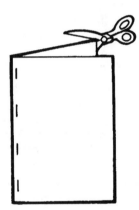

Rainforest Animals

❏ This animal is no bigger than a quarter.

❏ It has brightly colored skin that is poisonous.

❏ It hops.

What is it?

(*Answer.* A poison dart frog)

Using Maps to Enhance Reports

Maps can be used in a variety of ways to enhance written work. This activity will help your children identify different kinds of maps and learn how they are used.

Directions

1. Explain to the children that there are different kinds of maps that are used to show the location of countries, states, streets, buildings, and locations of events and different kinds of weather.

2. Explain that world maps show continents, countries, and bodies of water. Country and state maps show cities, highways, and landforms. City maps show streets and locations of buildings. Weather maps show the different kinds of weather in different areas.

3. Give each child a copy of "Types of Maps" (page 19) for identifying different kinds of maps.

4. Ask students to tell the kinds of things that could be shown on each kind of map.

5. To reinforce the different kinds and uses of maps, display a different kind of map each week. Post a list of questions about different locations beside the map and encourage children to use the map to answer the questions.

6. Continue to reinforce the skill by using your classroom computer to display a map from a CD-ROM encyclopedia. Encourage each child to view the map and familiarize himself or herself with the elements of the map.

7. For a homework assignment, instruct the children to look for maps in local newspapers. Have the children identify the types of maps found.

Cardinal Directions

Before creating maps of their own, your children will need to understand cardinal directions and how a compass rose is used to read a map.

Begin by displaying a large map. Draw students' attention to the compass rose. Explain that all maps have compass roses to show the directions north, south, east, and west. Familiarize your children with cardinal directions in your classroom by labeling appropriate walls of your classroom with signs labeled north, south, east, and west. Give your children directions such as "Stand near the south wall." Each time, have the children walk to the appropriate wall. Provide each child with a copy of "North, South, East, West" on page 20. Each child completes the page by writing the appropriate directions on each incomplete compass rose. Continue practice with directions by discussing medial directions—northeast, southwest, etc. Use page 21 for practice of this skill.

Types of Maps

Write the name of each map on the line below it. Use the Word Bank to help you.

1. _____

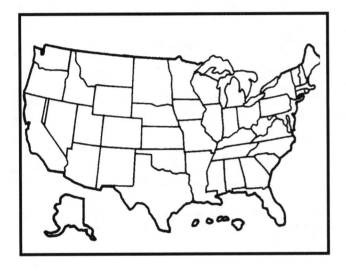

2. _____

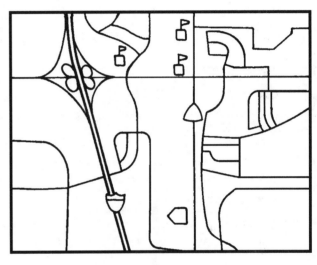

3. _____

4. _____

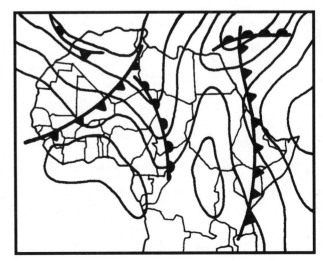

North, South, East, West

Fill in the missing directions. The first one has been done for you.

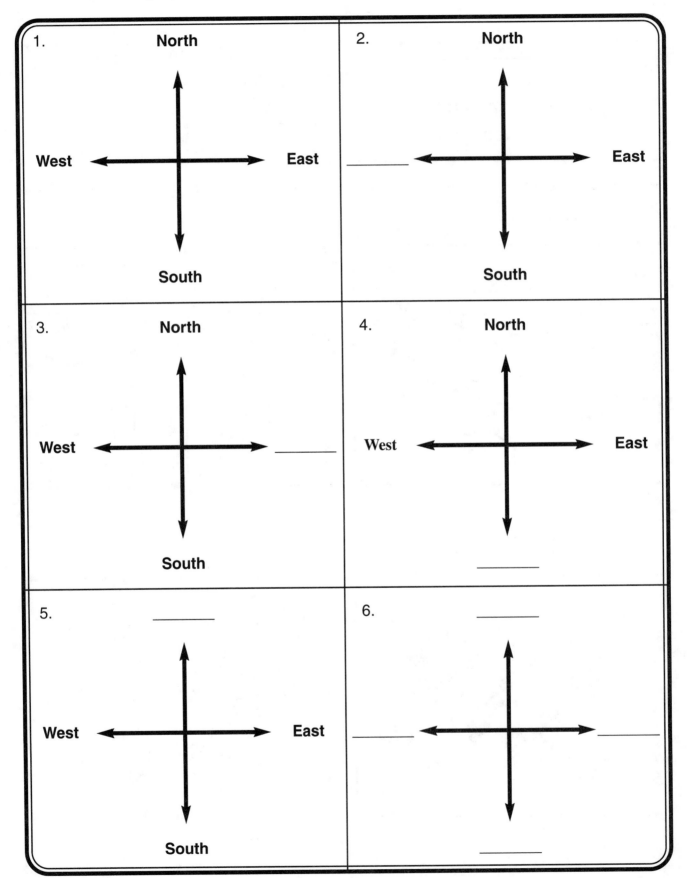

Complete the Compass Roses

Label the missing directions. The first one has been done for you.

❏ N = north	❏ NE = northeast
❏ S = south	❏ NW = northwest
❏ E = east	❏ SE = southeast
❏ W = west	❏ SW = southwest

1.

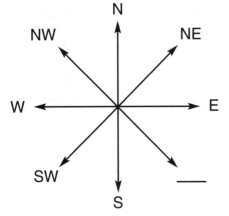

2.

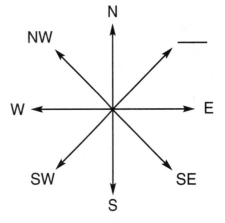

3.

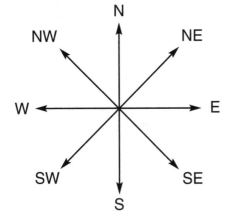

4.

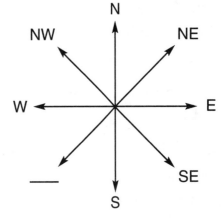

5.

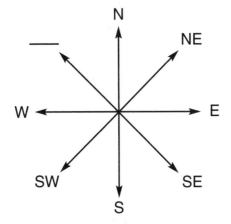

6.

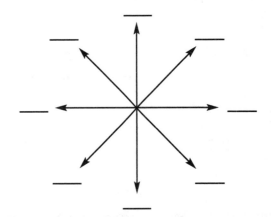

Reading and Making Map Keys

With this activity, your students will locate map keys, identify the symbols, and use the symbols to identify objects on maps.

Directions

1. Display a large map for the children to see.

2. Draw the children's attention to the key on the map and ask students if they can identify its use.

3. Explain that maps use symbols to represent objects such as lakes, rivers, highways, and cities. A map's key shows the symbols and tells what they mean.

4. Enlarge the map and key on page 23 and display it for the children to see. (You may want to duplicate a copy for each child.)

5. Ask the children to find the key. Then discuss each of the symbols in the key.

6. Ask the children to find the symbols on the map.

7. Have the children find the compass rose. Then ask them to find locations on the map using directions and symbols. Here are some suggested questions.

   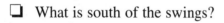

   ❑ What is north of the slide?

   ❑ What is south of the swings?

   ❑ What is west of the bench?

   ❑ What is south and east of the drinking fountain?

8. Invite the children to use the map to create their own questions to ask classmates.

9. Draw the children's attention to the fact that symbols on maps are very simple and do not have great detail. As a class, create a map of your classroom. Invite the children to think of simple ways to make symbols for objects such as desks, tables, bookcases, cabinets, etc.

Map and Key

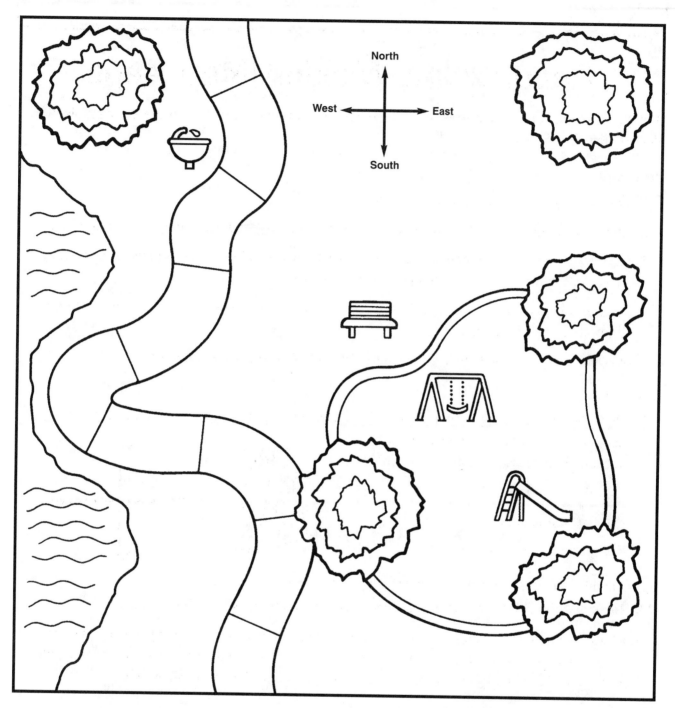

Using World Maps

Explain to your children that maps can be used to show locations related to a subject. For example, a world map could be used to highlight historic landmarks, vacation spots, or rainforests throughout the world. Display a large world map in your classroom and allow your children to view the oceans, continents, and countries shown. Provide the children with ideas for how the world map could be used to enhance their writing about a particular topic. Here are a few suggestions:

- ❏ travel destinations

- ❏ migration patterns of whales

- ❏ the location of a particular country

- ❏ the location of a particular animal's habitat

Provide each child with a copy of the world map on page 25 to accompany a written piece about a selected topic. Have each child color the map and highlight a particular area or areas that relate to his or her writing. Display completed work on a bulletin board entitled "Where in the World?"

Standards and Benchmarks: 1A, 1H, 4A, 4B

Using Weather Maps

Discuss with your children that weather maps can be used to show weather conditions that are typical in certain states or countries. Draw the weather symbols (page 27) on the chalkboard and have the children identify the weather condition represented by each.

Divide the children in pairs and provide each pair with a weather map cut from a local newspaper. Have each pair of students identify the weather symbols used and ask them to discuss the differences in weather throughout the county. Brainstorm a list of ways that weather maps could enhance written work. Be sure to include these suggestions.

- ❏ showing daily weather conditions in a state

- ❏ showing typical weather in different habitats

- ❏ reporting severe weather conditions in the country

Provide each child with a copy of "What's the Weather?" and the weather symbols on page 27. Have each child cut and paste weather symbols to the map as they relate to a particular weather-related topic. Then have the child write an article to accompany the map.

World Map

Color the map and label areas that relate to your topic.

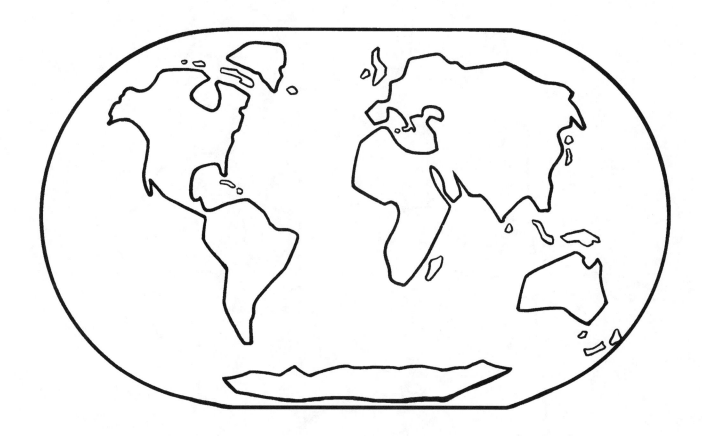

What's the Weather?

Weather Symbols

sun	clouds	rain	snow	wind
sun	clouds	rain	snow	wind
sun	clouds	rain	snow	wind
sun	clouds	rain	snow	wind
sun	clouds	rain	snow	wind
sun	clouds	rain	snow	wind
sun	clouds	rain	snow	wind
sun	clouds	rain	snow	wind

Picture Diagrams

The student will identify the usefulness of picture diagrams and make his or her own to accompany writing.

Procedure

1. Explain to your children that diagrams are used to make a subject easier to understand. One kind of diagram is a picture diagram.

2. Explain that a picture diagram can be used to show the parts of something, such as the body of a turtle, the parts of a toy, or the parts of a bicycle. For example, a person may not understand the meanings of the words "spokes" or "gears," but a look at the diagram below may make those words easier to understand.

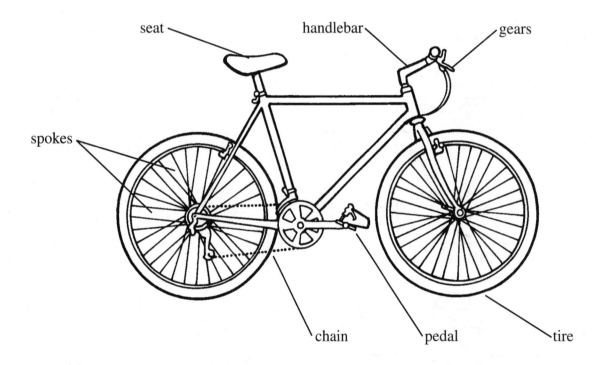

3. Provide each child with a copy of the diagram on page 29. As a class, discuss the diagram and then have each child answer the questions.

4. Have each child think about topics of interest to determine a writing piece that could use a picture diagram for enhancement.

5. Instruct each child to make a picture diagram to accompany a written piece.

6. Encourage children to share their diagrams with the class and explain how they think the diagram clarifies the writing.

7. For additional practice, have students look through books and magazines at home to find picture diagrams. How are these diagrams helpful in understanding what is written?

Picture Diagram

This is a diagram of a tree. Cut and glue the words below to label the picture.

roots	trunk	branch
fruit		leaves

Venn Diagrams

Directions

1. Explain to your children that Venn diagrams are used to show or to compare and contrast information. Venn diagrams, like picture diagrams, help a person to find information quickly.

2. Write the following list of information on the chalkboard or on chart paper:

   - Dogs play.
   - Dogs have fur.
   - Dogs bark.
   - Dogs need baths.
   - Dogs have tails.

   - Cats play.
   - Cats have fur.
   - Cats meow.
   - Cats wash themselves.
   - Cats have tails.

   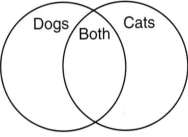

3. As a class, create a Venn diagram to show this information. Invite students to tell where each fact should be placed on the diagram.

4. Have each child complete "Making a Venn Diagram" on page 31.

5. Instruct each child to create his or her own Venn diagram using information on a research topic, such as whales and sharks.

6. Display each child's Venn diagram on a bulletin board entitled "Let's Compare!"

Standards and Benchmarks: 3A, 4A, 4B

Category Diagrams

Directions

1. Continue to discuss with your students the need to use visual materials to help a reader to better understand a subject. Another kind of diagram that can be used is a category diagram. For example, a report about healthy eating might discuss fruits and vegetables, meat, and starches. A category diagram could be used to show foods that fall into each category.

2. Write the words below on the chalkboard and explain that all of these items are foods. Some are fruits and vegetables, some are meats, and some are starches.

   | • apple | • cucumber | • chicken | • bread | • rice | • pork chops |
   | • carrot | • cereal | • fish | • turkey | • banana | • pasta |

3. Give each child a copy of the diagram on page 32 and have the children label the diagram and each category. Then have the child write the food words in the appropriate category blocks.

4. Instruct each child to create a category diagram showing different hobbies (sports, games, and crafts). Provide a copy of page 32 for each child's final diagram.

Making a Venn Diagram

Place the information below on the Venn diagram.

Candy Bars	**Ice Cream**
• different flavors	• different flavors
• served in wrappers	• served in cones or dishes
• tastes sweet	• tastes sweet
• can melt	• can be licked
• must be chewed	• is frozen
	• can melt

Comparing Candy Bars and Ice Cream

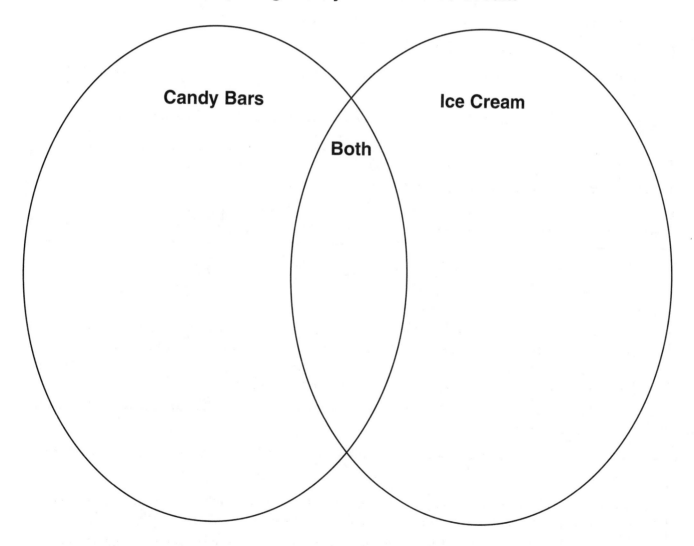

Candy Bars

Both

Ice Cream

Category Diagram

_____
(subject of the diagram)

(category 1)	(category 2)	(category 3)

Making Slideshow Presentations

Your children can create captivating presentations to display their writing and artistic ability, using computer-generated slideshows. This project has been created with *Kid Pix 2*. Similar slide shows can be created by using programs such as *HyperStudio* and *PowerPoint*.

Creating Pictures and Text

1. Using the "File" menu, drag to "New" to open a new document in *Kid Pix 2*.
2. Select the pencil or paintbrush from the tool bar; then click on the desired color to use. From the options bar below the screen, choose the desired pattern. Draw a picture and change colors, patterns, and tools, as desired.
3. Complete the picture by adding text. Open the "Goodies" menu at the top of the screen and drag to "Type Text."
4. Decide where to begin the sentence and click on the screen in that location. Type a sentence about the picture. If more than one line is needed for the sentence, it is necessary to press the "Return" key on the keyboard. Unlike a typical word-processing document, the text will not automatically shift to the next line. If you should happen to type beyond the screen, simply press the "Delete" key on the keyboard until the cursor can be seen again; then, press the "Return" key to move to the next line and continue typing.

Save the Picture and Create More

Using the "File" menu, "Save" the document. Create and save more pictures with text.

Creating a Slide Show

Follow the steps below to create a slide show of the saved pictures.

1. Open Slide Show from the main menu of *Kid Pix 2*. A page of trucks will appear on the screen.
2. Click the small icon of the slide at the base of the first truck. This will bring up a small screen asking which picture you want as the first slide in the slideshow.
3. Navigate to and double click on the desired picture. A thumbnail version of the picture will appear on the truck.
4. On the remaining trucks (or as many as you choose to use), continue selecting pictures in the same manner for the slide show.
5. Add sounds to each of the pictures by clicking on the music note on each truck. A menu of sounds will appear. You may preview the sounds before selecting the one you want. Add transitions between the pictures in your slide show by clicking on the transition box (to the right of the music note). A menu of transitions will appear. You may preview the transitions before selecting the one you want.
6. Play the slide show by clicking on the arrow button at the bottom of the slideshow screen.
7. Loop the slides together to be played over and over by clicking on the loop button (to the right of the arrow) at the bottom of the screen. To end the slide show, simply double click the mouse or press the "Command" and "Period" keys simultaneously on the keyboard.
8. "File…Save" the slideshow. This is a great project to show parents at Open House or at conferences.

Visual Aids for Journalism

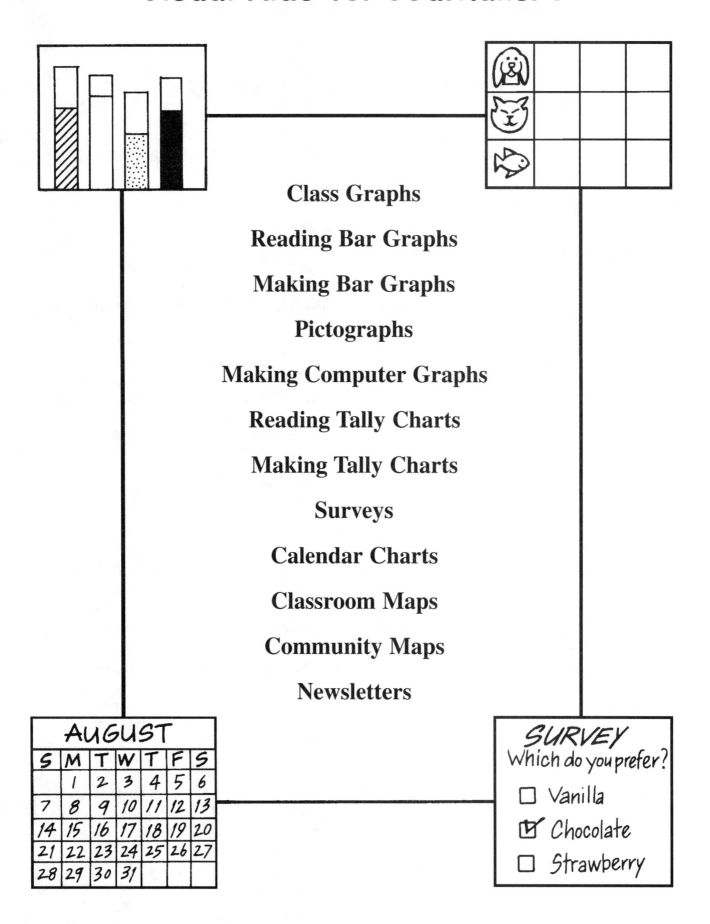

Class Graphs

Reading Bar Graphs

Making Bar Graphs

Pictographs

Making Computer Graphs

Reading Tally Charts

Making Tally Charts

Surveys

Calendar Charts

Classroom Maps

Community Maps

Newsletters

AUGUST

S	M	T	W	T	F	S
	1	2	3	4	5	6
7	8	9	10	11	12	13
14	15	16	17	18	19	20
21	22	23	24	25	26	27
28	29	30	31			

SURVEY
Which do you prefer?

☐ Vanilla

☑ Chocolate

☐ Strawberry

Class Graphs

Give your children an introductory experience in making graphs with these group activities.

Stack It Up

For this activity, you'll need a supply of books (one per child) that are all approximately the same thickness. Select a topic for rating, such as today's lunch, a familiar movie or book, or a class activity. Ask the children to think about the things they liked or disliked about the topic and have them each rate it on the following scale: Great, Okay, and Bad. Select a designated place on the floor for each rating category. Then ask each child to stack a book in one of the piles according to his or her rating choice. When all of the books are piled up, ask the children questions about this three-dimensional graph, such as the following:

- ❑ How did most of the children feel about the topic?
- ❑ Did more children like it or dislike it?
- ❑ How many children thought it was great?

That's Me!

Here's another great way to rate topics with your class. Select related topics to rate, such as baseball vs. soccer, movies vs. video games, or apples vs. bananas. Ask each child to choose a favorite and encourage him or her to think of several reasons why it is his or her favorite. Create and label a graph. To indicate a favorite, each child draws a self-portrait on a two-inch (5 cm) construction-paper square and attaches it in the row beside his or her favorite item.

Clothespin Graph

This graphing activity gives your children the opportunity to compare things. Begin by reading two books. Ask the children to think about the story events and characters. Which book was more entertaining? Which book had better illustrations? Create a clothespin graph by dividing a posterboard into two columns. Label the top of each column with the title of one of the books. Then have each child clip a clothespin onto the side labeled with his or her favorite book. Calculate the total number of children who selected each book and encourage them to share the reasons they made their choices. See the list below for other items to compare.

- art class and music class
- seasons
- outdoor activities
- food items

- holidays
- reading class and math class
- vacation spots
- restaurants

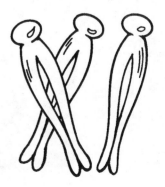

Reading Bar Graphs

This activity helps your children learn to read bar graphs and to understand how they can be used to enhance their written work.

Procedure

1. Begin the lesson by asking each child to think of his or her favorite flavor of ice cream. You may want to offer four or five choices, such as "Chocolate," "Vanilla," "Strawberry," and "Other."

2. Count the responses and make a list similar to the one below.

   Chocolate—10   Strawberry—2

   Vanilla—3   Other—5

3. Explain that this information can be placed on a bar graph to make it easier to read.

4. Create a bar graph (either vertically or horizontally) using the gathered responses. See the examples below.

Vertical
Favorite Ice Cream

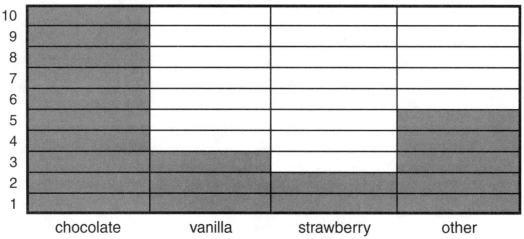

Horizontal
Favorite Ice Cream

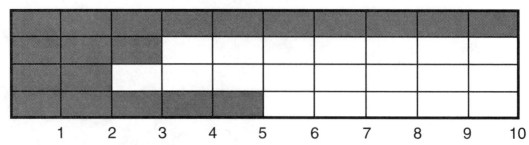

Reading Bar Graphs *(cont.)*

5. Draw the children's attention to the numbers column/row and the category row/column. Then show them how to view the bars in order to determine the number of children who like each flavor. Explain that it is not necessary to count each section of a bar in order to determine the number, but rather simply find the number that is beside the top (or end) of each bar.

6. Ask the children questions and have them use the graph or the original list to determine the answers.

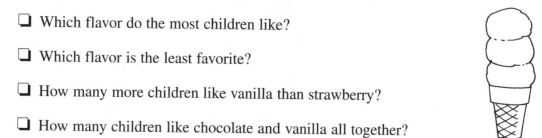

   ❏ Which flavor do the most children like?

   ❏ Which flavor is the least favorite?

   ❏ How many more children like vanilla than strawberry?

   ❏ How many children like chocolate and vanilla all together?

7. Have the children tell whether the list or the graph was easier to use when determining the answers.

8. Have the children complete the lesson worksheets on pages 38 and 39. The first page contains a vertical bar graph and the second contains a horizontal bar graph. Explain that either type can be used to convey similar information.

9. After completing the lesson worksheets, ask the children to think of ways that bar graphs could be used in written work. If desired, show the children a magazine or newspaper article containing a bar graph. Read all or some of the article and allow the children to view and discuss the graph.

10. On a bulletin board, display a large bar graph. Attach question cards (pertaining to the graph) to the bulletin board around the graph. Encourage the children to read the graph and determine the answers.

11. Make and display a bar graph using the graph feature of a spreadsheet program or find a graph on the Internet to display. Invite the children to read and discuss the graph.

Reading a Vertical Bar Graph

Use the graph to answer the questions.

Favorite Wild Animals

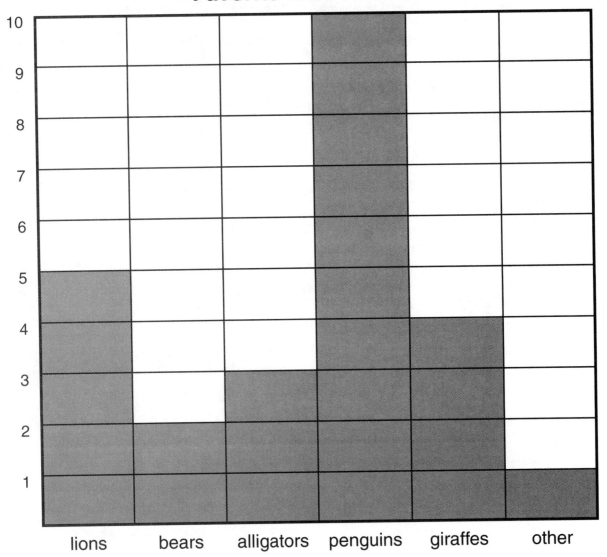

1. How many children like lions? _____

2. How many children like penguins? _____

3. How many children like giraffes? _____

4. How many children like bears? _____

5. Do more children like alligators or penguins? _____

6. How many children like either bears or giraffes? _____

Reading a Horizontal Bar Graph

Use the graph to answer the questions.

Afterschool Activities

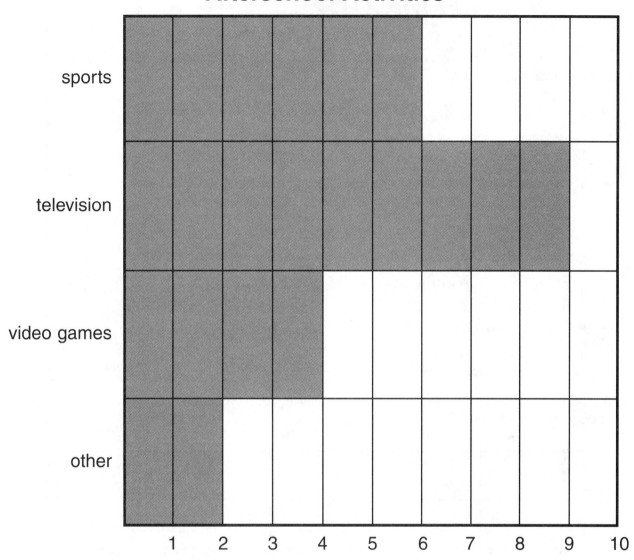

1. How many children like to play sports after school? _____

2. How many children like to watch television? _____

3. How many children like to play video games? _____

4. How many children like to do other kinds of activities? _____

5. Do more children like to play sports or watch television? _____

6. Do less children like to play video games or play sports? _____

Making Bar Graphs

Now it's time to make bar graphs to accompany articles. Your children can make horizontal and vertical bar graphs about selected topics.

Procedure

1. Begin by reviewing the previous lesson about reading bar graphs. Remind the children that bar graphs can be made vertically or horizontally.

2. Ask the children to tell why bar graphs are easier to read than lists of information. (You may want to refresh their memories by displaying a list of information and an accompanying graph.)

3. Display a graph outline and the list of information below.

Number of Children in Second Grade

Mrs. Prior's class—22   Mrs. Schutter's class—24

Ms. Christiansen's class—21   Miss Smith's class—23

Ms. Novy's class—22

---

4. As a class, use the information to create a vertical or a horizontal bar graph, showing the number of children in each class.

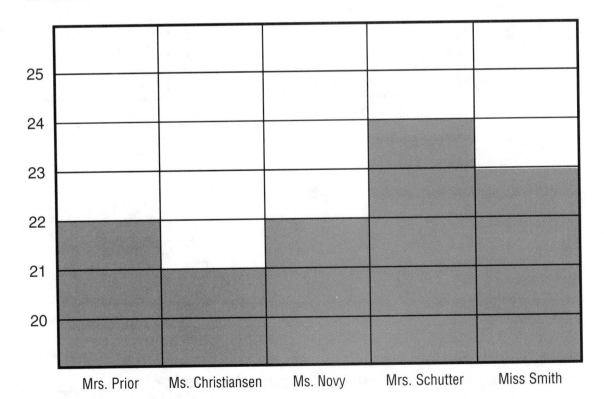

Making Bar Graphs *(cont.)*

5. Ask the following questions about the graph:

    ❏ How many children are in Mrs. Schutter's class?

    ❏ How many children are in Mrs. Prior's class?

    ❏ Which two teachers have the same number of children in class?

6. Invite the children to add to the question list by creating questions of their own that could be answered by the graph.

7. Have the children complete the lesson worksheets on pages 42 and 43. The children are asked to use sets of information to label and create vertical and horizontal bar graphs.

8. After completing the lesson worksheets, ask the children to think of ways that bar graphs could be used in written work. Examples include favorite school lunches, favorite authors, etc.

9. Have each child write an informational paragraph and make a graph to go with it.

10. Allow the children to edit and recopy their written work. Display each child's writing and graph on a bulletin board entitled "First-Class Graphs."

11. Computer Project: Show the children how to make their own graphs using a computer spreadsheet program. See "Making Computer Graphs" (page 48) for easy-to-follow steps.

Making a Vertical Bar Graph

Use the information below to make a vertical bar graph.

> **Our Favorite Fruit**
>
> apples—6   grapes—4
> bananas—3   strawberries—7

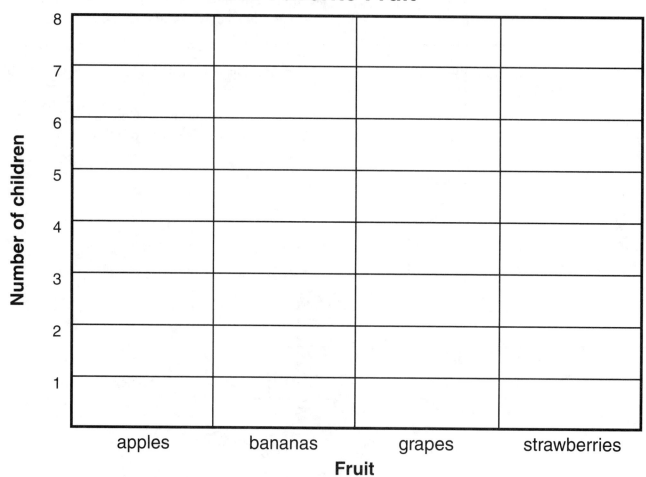

Our Favorite Fruit

1. How many children like strawberries? _____

2. How many children like apples? _____

3. Do more children like grapes or bananas? _____

Write two more questions for the graph.

_____

_____

Making a Horizontal Bar Graph

Use the information below to label and create a horizontal bar graph.

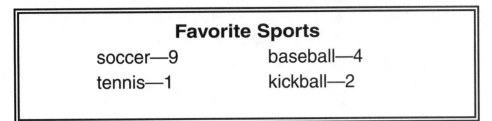

Favorite Sports

soccer—9   baseball—4
tennis—1   kickball—2

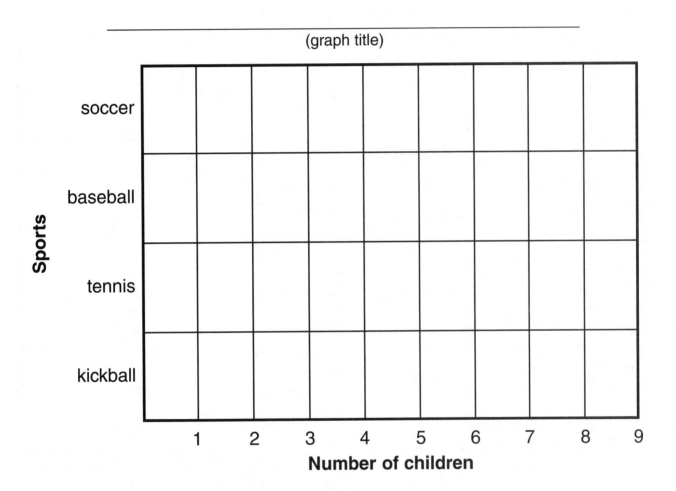

1. Which sport do most children like? _____

2. How many children like to play kickball? _____

3. How many like to play tennis? _____

Write two more questions for this graph.

_____

_____

Pictographs

Help your children understand how to read pictographs and realize their usefulness in writing.

Procedure

1. Draw the pictograph and key below on the chalkboard. Explain to the children that the key shows that each face represents two people. Ask the children questions based on the graph.

Sample Pictograph

candy bars | 😊 | 😊 | 😊 | (| | | | |
cake | 😊 | 😊 | | | | | | |
ice cream | 😊 | 😊 | 😊 | 😊 | 😊 | 😊 | 😊 | |

     2   4   6   8   10   12   14   16

Key

😊 = two people

2. Draw their attention to the half face in the candy bar row. Ask the children what they think that means. Explain that since each face represents two people, a half face represents one person.

3. Be certain that students understand that pictographs are also known as picture graphs. Also, make sure that students understand how the key is used.

4. Provide each child with a copy of "Reading a Pictograph" on page 45 for completion.

5. Brainstorm with students a list of symbols that might be used in a pictograph, such as trees, flowers, cars, people, houses, or animals. Have each student choose a topic and symbol and practice drawing his or her symbol. Some sample topics might include trees to represent how many different kinds of trees are on the school grounds or people to represent how many siblings each student in the class has.

6. Distribute copies of the pictograph outline and symbols on pages 46 and 47. Select a topic for the graph. (See suggestions below.) Have each child use the tally chart on page 53 to gather information. Then have each child create a graph by labeling the categories and cutting and pasting symbols appropriately.

Graph Ideas

• classmates' pets   • favorite sports   • types of plants on the school grounds

---

7. Have each child write a short article telling about the graph.

8. If desired, use the graphics library of a word-processing program to find interesting symbols to print for pictographs.

9. Extend practice of this skill by having the children look through magazines and newspapers at home for examples of pictographs. Encourage them to bring copies to school to share.

Reading a Pictograph

Use the graph to answer the questions.

Animals at the Zoo

Key

each picture = 2 animals

1. How many zebras are at the zoo? _____

2. How many lions are there? _____

3. How many monkeys are there? _____

4. Are there more elephants or lions? _____

5. Are there less monkeys or zebras? _____

Making a Pictograph

Use the outline below to make a pictograph. Don't forget to make a key.

_____

(graph title)

Key

Pictograph Symbols

Making Computer Graphs

Your children can gather information and display it using attractive computer-generated graphs. These can be used to accompany articles or displayed in newsletters. This project has been created using *AppleWorks* or *ClarisWorks* with additional directions for *Microsoft Excel* and *Word 98* in parentheses.

Gather Information

1. Review with your children the use of graphs and how to conduct surveys. Here are some ideas for graphs.

   ❑ class favorites (pets, food, games, weekend activities)

   ❑ daily high temperatures

   ❑ types of weather in a given month

   ❑ number of children buying and bringing lunch

2. Have the children record information on the tally sheet on page 53.

Create a Spreadsheet

Perform the following procedures to create a spreadsheet of the gathered information.

1. Click to open *AppleWorks*. Then open the "File" menu and drag to "New" to open a new document. Select "Spreadsheet" and click "OK." (For *Excel*, simply double click to open the program.)

2. Input the data into the spreadsheet cells. For example, a graph about favorite pets might have the headings "Dogs," "Cats," "Fish," and "Hamsters." Type a different animal name in the first cell of columns A through D. Below each heading, numerically list the number of children who selected that animal as his or her favorite.

3. Click "Save" under the "File" menu to save this spreadsheet.

Create a Graph

Use the following steps to create a graph of the information from the spreadsheet.

1. Click and drag to highlight the data on the spreadsheet.

2. Still in the spreadsheet file, click on "Options" and drag to "Make Chart." (*Excel* users, click on "Chart Wizard" in the top toolbar.) A screen will appear, showing several different kinds of graphs. Click the desired type of graph to represent the data. (For *Excel*, click "Next." Decide whether to use rows or columns and click "Next" again.)

Making Computer Graphs *(cont.)*

3. The completed graph will have a legend box labeled "Series 1," unless modifications are made. To remove the legend box, select "Labels" and click on the X. (*Excel* users will see a variety of tabs. Select "Legends" and then uncheck the "Show Legend" box.)

4. A title can also be created for the graph at this point. (*Excel* users will find a "Titles" tab. See step three.)

Import the Graph into Word Processing

You can easily import the graph from the spreadsheet file to a word processing document.

1. In order to import the graph, the image must be highlighted. The graph is highlighted if a dark square can be seen at each corner. If the dark squares are not present, click within the graph area one time. Go to the "Edit" menu and drag down to "Copy." This will make a copy of the graph so it can be pasted onto a word-processing document.

2. Go to "File" and drag to "New" to open a new document. Select "Word Processing" and then click "OK." (*Excel* users should exit the program and open a *Word 98* word-processing document.)

3. From the "Edit" menu, drag to "Paste" and the graph will appear at the top of the page.

4. To change the size of the graph, click once on the image, then click on the dark square in the lower right corner and drag to create the desired size. (For *Excel*, use the top left square.)

Adding Text

Have each child tell about his or her graph and explain what it indicates about the gathered information.

1. Click in the area below the graph or press the Return key to reveal the cursor.

2. Type a few sentences telling about the graph and the information indicated on it.

3. When the writing is complete, "File…Save" the document.

Printing the Project

Make any desired changes before printing the document. If the graph should be accidentally deleted, immediately select "Undo" from the "Edit" menu and the graph will reappear. "File…Print" the document and display it.

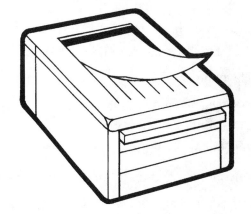

Reading Tally Charts

Tally charts are a great way for young children to record information. These charts can be used to accompany their personally written articles. With the next three lessons, your children will learn how to gather information, read charts, and create their own charts using tally marks.

Procedure

1. Discuss with your children that charts are used to gather or show different kinds of information. A tally chart is one kind of chart that can be used.

2. Draw the tally chart below on a sheet of chart paper. Display the chart for the children and ask them to tell what it shows.

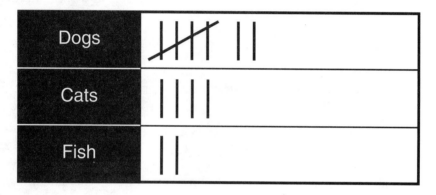

3. Draw the children's attention to the use of tally marks on the chart. Lead them into a discussion about the way the marks are grouped. Ask them to tell why they think the marks are grouped in fives.

4. Ask the children to identify the elements of the chart. Then ask the following questions:
    - ❏ How many children like dogs the best?
    - ❏ How many children like fish?
    - ❏ Do more children like fish or cats?

5. Have the children brainstorm different kinds of information that could be gathered on tally charts.

6. Have each child complete "Making Tally Marks" on page 51 in preparation for the tally chart project in the next lesson.

7. Instruct each child to write an additional question that could be answered by the tally chart.

8. Encourage children to share their questions for classmates to answer.

9. For additional practice, instruct each child to make a simple tally chart about favorite foods. Have them gather information from family members and friends.

10. Create a bulletin-board display to exhibit each child's work.

11. Using a drawing program, show your children how to make tally marks by drawing four straight lines and one diagonal line across them.

Making Tally Marks

When making a tally chart, you make a line for everything you count. To make it easier to read, every fifth mark is crossed over the four marks that come before it.

Count each set of tally marks below and write how many there are.

1. |||| _____

2.  _____

3. || _____

4. ||| | _____

5.  || _____

6. | _____

7. ||| ||| _____

8. ||| |||| _____

Write tally marks to show each number below.

9. 5 _____

10. 2 _____

11. 6 _____

12. 9 _____

13. 10 _____

14. 3 _____

15. 7 _____

16. 8 _____

Making Tally Charts

Your children will select information for tally charts. They will then create their own charts to accompany written work.

Procedure

1. Review the use of tally charts in recording and showing information. Explain to your children that using a tally chart (with marks grouped in fives) allows a reader to gather information quickly.

2. Explain that tally charts can be used when surveying people. For example, you might want to know which subject is the class favorite. A tally mark would be made to show each child's vote. Tally charts can also be used for counting things. For example, you may want to know how many classmates have brothers and/or sisters. Tally marks would be used to show the number of siblings.

3. Have each child complete the chart on page 53 by selecting a topic of interest and surveying or counting in order to complete it.

Favorite Sandwich
(subject)

Choices	Tally Marks
Tuna	III
Peanut Butter and Jelly	II
Turkey	H̶I̶I̶I̶ I
B. L. T.	IIII
Ham and Cheese	II

4. Instruct each child to write a paragraph about the information gathered on his or her tally chart.

5. Have each child mount his or her written piece and tally chart on a backing of colored construction paper for display.

6. Assist children in making computer-generated labels for their charts.

Making a Tally Chart

Decide on the information you would like to gather on your tally chart. Write a title on the chart and label the left column. Use tally marks to show the information.

_____
(subject)

Choices	Tally Marks

Tell something that the chart shows.

_____

What did you learn from your chart?

_____

Surveys

Now that your children understand how to read and make tally charts, they're ready to begin conducting surveys. With this lesson, your children will select types of charts or graphs for presenting the survey information.

Procedure

1. Explain to your children that charts and graphs are great ways to show information to others.

2. Review the kinds of charts and graphs that they have already learned to read and make.

3. Next, explain to students that information for charts and graphs can often be gathered in the form of a survey. A simple survey usually consists of one question (sometimes more) on a particular topic. Share some of the topics below.

   ❏ favorite subject in school   ❏ favorite day of the week

   ❏ favorite afterschool activity   ❏ favorite season

4. Select one of these topics and conduct a quick survey with your students. Draw a simple chart for recording responses and explain how to tally similar responses.

5. Then demonstrate how the information from the tally chart can be transferred to make a chart or a graph.

6. Provide each child with a copy of "Conducting a Survey" on page 55 and have him or her create a survey to conduct in class.

7. Have children work together to assist each other in transferring their survey information to charts and graphs.

8. Instruct each child to write about the process of making and conducting surveys. Then have the child write about what he or she has learned about how charts and graphs can be used to reflect information.

9. For additional practice, have each child conduct a survey at home on a topic of interest and graph or chart the results to share at school.

10. Display each child's completed chart or graph and written work and encourage classmates to read them.

11. Have students type their surveys using a word-processing program. Challenge interested students to make computer-generated graphs to show the results of their surveys. (See "Making Computer Graphs" on pages 48 and 49 for assistance.)

Conducting a Survey

What question will you ask your classmates? _____

_____

Write the title of your survey above the tally chart.

Then write the choices in the left column.

_____
(title)

_____ Total: _____

_____ Total: _____

_____ Total: _____

_____ Total: _____

_____ Total: _____

_____ Total: _____

Do you plan to use a chart, a bar graph, a line graph, or a pie graph?

_____

Draw your graph on a separate piece of paper.

Standards and Benchmarks: 1H

Calendar Charts

This activity helps your children to understand how calendars are used to chart information.

Procedure

1. Explain to the children that there are many different kinds of charts and that a calendar is a kind of chart that not only shows the date, but also charts information.

2. Display the following information on a sheet of chart paper:

   Monday—music lesson @ 3:30   Thursday—softball practice @ 3:00
   Tuesday—softball practice @ 3:00   Saturday—art lesson @ 10:00

3. Display a weekly calendar (as shown below) and demonstrate how to place the information on it.

S	M	T	W	Th	F	Sat

4. Brainstorm a list of ideas for how a calendar could be used to chart information. See the list of suggestions below.

   ❏ afterschool events and activities
   ❏ weather for a particular month
   ❏ spelling test dates
   ❏ dates and times of educational television shows

5. Provide each child with a copy of "Read a Calendar" on page 57 to complete.

6. Have each child write a list of ideas for creating calendars to show information.

7. Display a large drawing of a monthly calendar and have each child write the days he or she participates in special afterschool activities. Discuss how calendars can be helpful in displaying and scheduling information.

8. Provide copies of the blank calendar on page 58. Have each child determine an article to write concerning dates and times of selected activities. Have the child write the article and then complete the calendar accordingly.

9. Computer Activity: Many computer programs have a feature for creating calendars. For an additional activity, assist the children in making calendars of their daily events.

Read a Calendar

Use the calendar to answer the questions below.

School Events in May

Sunday	Monday	Tuesday	Wed.	Thurs.	Friday	Saturday
	1	2 Music Performance	3	4	5	6
7	8	9	10	11	12	13 Carnival
14 Mother's Day	15	16	17	18 Class Party	19 Last Day of School	20
21	22	23	24	25	26	27
28	29	30	31 Memorial Day			

1. On what day of the week is Memorial Day? _____

2. On what date is Mother's Day? _____

3. When is the last day of school? _____

4. On what day of the week is the school carnival? _____

5. What date is the music performance? _____

6. On what day of the week is the class party? _____

Calendar Template

_____

(month)

Sunday	Monday	Tuesday	Wed.	Thurs.	Friday	Saturday

Classroom Maps

When writing about classroom events and activities, your children may want to use classroom maps to show where the activities took place.

Directions

1. Review with your children the usefulness of maps and explain that a map can be made to represent many different places, including the classroom.

2. Begin by drawing a map of an area of your home, such as the living room. Use basic symbols, such as circles, squares, rectangles, etc., to represent couches, chairs, tables, and the television set. Include a compass rose and a map key to show what the symbols represent.

3. Ask the children several questions about your map, such as the following:

   ❑ How many chairs are in the living room?
   ❑ Is the television closer to the table or the couch?
   ❑ In what direction is the kitchen from the living room?
   ❑ What piece of furniture is east of the couch?

4. Provide the children with copies of the map worksheet on page 60 to complete.

5. Ask the children to look around the room, taking note of the positions of the desks, tables, classroom library, sink, cabinets, and other items. Decide as a class the kinds of symbols that should be used to represent these objects. Write the symbols and what they could represent on the chalkboard.

6. Give each child a sheet of paper and have him or her create a map of the classroom, including a compass rose and a map key. Encourage each child to make each symbol a different color to add interest.

7. Have the children think of articles that they would like to write about the classroom. See the suggestions below.

   ❑ where the children sit
   ❑ rotation of classroom learning centers
   ❑ an interesting science experiment
   ❑ story about the class pet

8. Explain that a classroom map can accompany a story to show the reader where things are located in the room.

9. Instruct each child to select a class-related topic to write about to accompany his or her map.

Reading a Classroom Map

Use the map and key to answer the questions below.

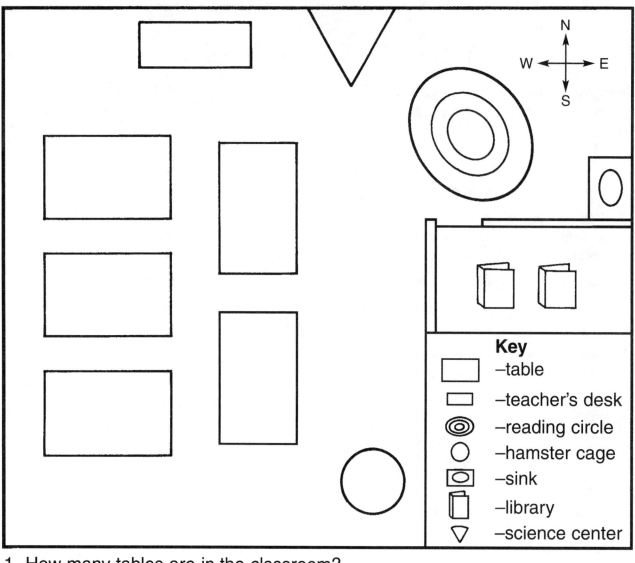

Key
- ▭ –table
- ▭ –teacher's desk
- ◎ –reading circle
- ○ –hamster cage
- ▣ –sink
- ▯ –library
- ▽ –science center

1. How many tables are in the classroom?

_____

2. Along which wall is the teacher's desk?

_____

3. What area is north of the classroom library?

_____

4. The reading circle is west of what area?

_____

5. Is the hamster cage closer to the science center or the reading circle?

_____

Community Maps

Add visual appeal to articles about community areas and events by making community maps.

Directions

1. Review with your children the use of maps to accompany written work.

2. Brainstorm with your children some of the topics they could write about relating to their local community, such as sporting events, carnivals, neighborhood picnics, nearby restaurants, or movie theaters.

3. Provide each child with a copy of the map worksheet on page 62 for completion. Remind the children to use the compass rose and the map key to assist in reading the map. Draw the children's attention to the use of basic symbols on the map.

4. As a class, create a map of your community. Include the school, nearby streets, familiar stores and restaurants, and parks. Create the map on a sheet of chart paper for all to see.

5. Discuss the areas of the map and ask the children questions about the map. Explain that an article could be written about a carnival at the school. A map could accompany the article to show a person how to find it.

6. Provide each child with a large sheet of construction paper and the map symbols on page 63.

7. Have each child recreate the community map by cutting and gluing the symbols in the appropriate positions on the map. Remind the child to glue on the compass rose and create a map key. Encourage each child to create other symbols, if needed.

  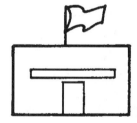 

8. Instruct each child to write an article about a community-related topic.

9. Allow the children to share their completed maps and articles with classmates.

10. Display the maps on a bulletin board entitled "Community Events."

Reading a Community Map

Use the map to answer the questions below.

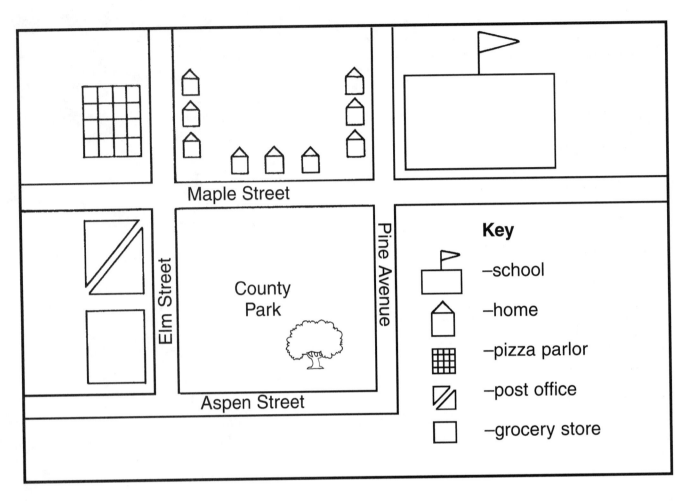

1. On what street corner is the school located? _____

_____

_____

2. What building is directly north of the post office? _____

3. What four streets surround the park? _____

_____

_____

4. Is the grocery store closer to the park or the school? _____

Community Map Symbols

Newsletters

Your students can create a computer-generated newsletter to display their completed articles. The following project requires *AppleWorks* (*ClarisWorks*) for completion; however, a similar newsletter can be created using Microsoft Word's Newsletter Wizard feature. If you do not have access to computers, you can duplicate the template on page 66 and have the children write the newsletters by hand.

Newsletter Template

1. Designing a newsletter involves several procedures. In order to simplify this project for students, follow the directions below to create a newsletter template that can be used by students in writing their own newsletters.

2. Select "File...New" to open a new document in *AppleWorks*.

3. From the resulting screen, click the box to "Use Assistant or Stationery."

4. Select "Newsletter" and click "OK."

5. The Newsletter Assistant will appear. Follow the series of steps on the screen to create the desired newsletter. (You will be asked to click "Next" after each choice made in creating the newsletter.)

6. Click "Create" to assemble the newsletter template. After a brief pause, the newsletter will be created and a screen of "Tips & Hints" will appear. You may choose to read or print the tips. After doing this, "File...Close" the "Tips & Hints" window.

7. To create a blank graphics box (instead of the box with crossed lines), select "New View" from the "Window" menu (or the "View" menu in *ClarisWorks*). Click on the rectangle tool on the left side of the newsletter. Then drag the cursor over the crossed box to create a blank box.

8. Now, "File...Save" the document as a template and have the children use this outline to create their own newsletters.

Ideas for the Newsletter

Generate discussion among your students about what might be included in their newsletter. Ideas could include the following:

- school events

- articles about research topics

- weekly classroom activities and accomplishments

Newsletters *(cont.)*

Writing the Newsletter

Open the newsletter template, select "File…Save As," and enter the child's name. Type a headline for each article in the chosen location. Next, type each article beneath its headline. Adjust the size of the type by highlighting the text (click and drag over the text); then go to "Size" and drag to the desired point size. Adjust the style of the text such as boldface type, italics, etc., by clicking and dragging to highlight the text and selecting from the "Style" menu.

Adding Graphics

AppleWorks provides a library of graphics that can be used in this project to add visual appeal.

1. The box on the newsletter is the perfect place to add graphics. To do this, go to the "File" menu and drag to "Library."

2. A small menu of weather graphics will appear. Select the desired picture and click "Use." The picture will appear on the newsletter.

3. Click on the picture and drag it to the graphics box. The size can easily be adjusted by clicking and dragging the dark square in the lower right corner of the graphic.

Save and Print

Using the "File" menu, drag to "Save" in order to save the newsletter. If printing only one of the pages of the newsletter, go to the "File" menu and select "Print." Then, in the print window, type "1" after the word "From" and "1" after the word "To."

Newsletter Template

Visuals for Book Reports

Story Events

Character Collage

Character Puzzles

Story Stew

Finger Puppets

Book Report Block

Story Setting

Story Picture Frame

Story Menus

Story Events

Here's an innovative way for your children to tell about books they have read.

Procedure

1. After reading a book, provide each child with a supply of 3" x 2" (8 cm x 5 cm) cards.

2. On the front of each card, the child writes a different question about the story. See the list below for question ideas.

3. On the back of each card, the child writes the answer to the question.

4. Provide each child with a copy of the game board on page 69. The child writes the title and author of the book on the designated lines.

5. Have the child color scenes from the story around the game path. If desired, laminate the game board and cards or attach them to sturdy paper.

6. Choose small objects for game pieces, such as coins or plastic chips.

7. To play, two classmates read the book. Next, they place the game board on a flat surface and stack the question cards faceup on the board. Then, they follow the directions on the game board to play. The first player to reach "Finish" is the winner.

Examples of Game Cards

What does the main character look like?	What are three events that take place in the story?	Describe the main character's home.
What is the main problem in the story?	What obstacles does the main character face?	How is the main problem in the story resolved?
Who helps the main character solve the problem?	What are the main character's feelings about the problem?	Where does the story take place?

Story Events *(cont.)*

Game Board

_____

(book title)

_____

(author)

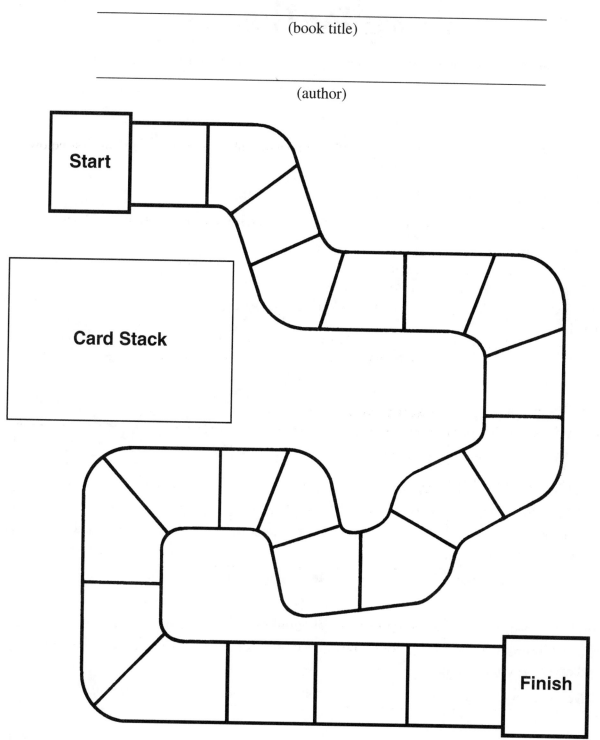

Directions

Player 1 reads the top card in the stack and answers the question. If correct, he or she moves ahead one space. Then, it's Player 2's turn. The first player to reach "Finish" is the winner.

Character Collage

Your students can create simple and decorative collages to accompany written work about book characters.

Materials

- discarded magazines
- scissors
- glue
- two different colors of 9" x 13" (22.8 cm x 32.9 cm) sheets of construction paper
- crayons or markers

Directions

1. After reading a book, ask each child to think about the main character. Ask the following questions:

   - What does the character look like?
   - Was he or she a girl, a boy, or an animal?
   - Does he or she wear glasses?
   - What does the character like to do?
   - Does the character have a hobby?
   - Does he or she have a favorite food?
   - Does he or she have friends?

   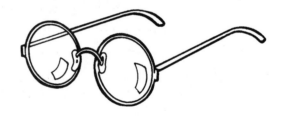

2. Distribute discarded magazines and have each child look for and cut out pictures and words that relate to the character.

3. Have each child glue the pictures and words in collage form to one of the sheets of construction paper.

4. Cut out the center of the second sheet of construction paper, leaving a 1" (2.5 cm) frame.

5. Glue the frame atop the collage. Use crayons or markers to write the name of the book, author, and character on the frame.

6. Have each child write a summary of the story to attach beneath the collage for display.

Character Puzzles

This project is a great way for your children to demonstrate their knowledge of characters in books they have read.

Materials

- children's book with two or more characters
- puzzle patterns (page 72)
- crayons
- scissors
- an envelope or a resealable plastic bag

Directions

1. Have each child read a book with two or more characters.

2. Ask the children to think about the likes and dislikes of the characters.

3. Provide each child with a copy of the puzzle patterns on page 72.

4. On the lower portion of each puzzle set, the child colors a picture of a character. (The same character can be used more than once.)

5. On the upper portion of each puzzle set, the child colors something related to the character, such as a favorite friend, a favorite activity, a fear, or something he or she dislikes.

6. After completing the puzzle drawings, the child cuts out the pieces and places them in an envelope or a resealable plastic bag.

7. Have each child display the book he or she read along with the puzzle pieces and a story write-up.

8. Encourage classmates to read the book and match the puzzle pieces to show their knowledge of the characters in the book.

Puzzle Patterns

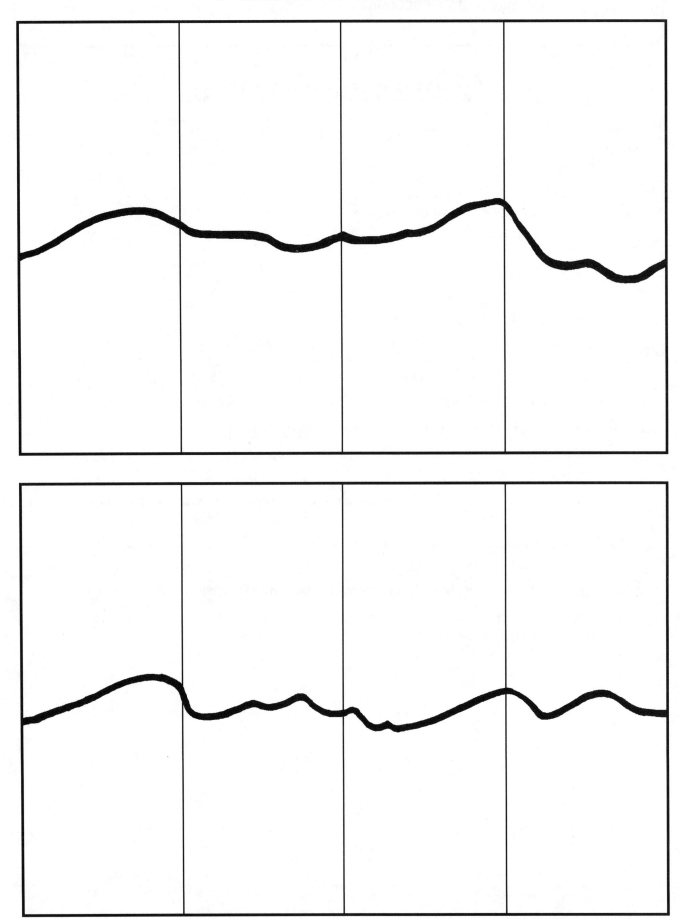

Story Stew

Here's a fun way for the children to tell classmates about books they have read.

Materials

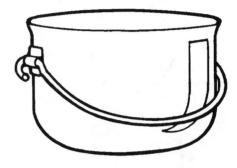

- children's book
- large stew pot
- variety of gathered items relating to the story
- wooden spoon or other stirring utensil
- apron and chef's hat (optional)

Directions

1. After reading a book, have each child think about the characters and events of the story.

2. Have each child gather pictures and objects that relate to the story. For example, after reading *A Chair for my Mother* by Vera B. Williams, the child might gather the following items:

   - a dollhouse chair
   - coins
   - a restaurant menu
   - a picture of a fire
   - a picture or figurine of a young woman, a girl, and an older woman

3. Place the items on a table beside the stew pot and wooden spoon.

4. To present the book, a child wears an apron and chef's hat (optional). He or she begins by saying, "I'm going to tell you about a book I read." He or she then tells about each object and how it relates to the story and places it in the pot.

5. After all the objects have been added to the pot, the child pretends to stir the items in the pot and concludes by saying, "Mix them all together and you get [name of book] by [name of author]."

Finger Puppets

After reading a story, have your children make finger puppets of the characters. Provide each child with the finger puppet patterns on page 74. The child colors a different story character on each pattern, cuts it out, and tapes the puppets around a finger. Have each child write a script for the character puppets. Allow him or her to stand before the class and use the puppets to tell about the story from the characters' points of view.

Finger Puppets

Color a puppet for each of the main characters of a book. Cut out the puppets and tape the tabs together so the puppet fits snugly on a finger.

Standards and Benchmarks: 1G, 1H, 3B

Book Report Block

A book report can be displayed creatively by making a book report block. After reading a book, have each child think about the following questions:

- What happened in the story?
- Who was the main character?
- Where did the story take place?
- What was the problem in the story?

- How was the problem solved?
- What was your favorite part of the story?
- Would you recommend this story to a friend?

Provide each child with a book report block pattern (page 76). The child writes about and illustrates parts of the story. Display completed cubes on a table, using children's letter blocks to create a title.

Standards and Benchmarks: 1G, 1H

Story Setting

As your children read, encourage them to think about the details of a story's setting. Use the list below to help.

- ❑ Where does the story take place?
- ❑ Is it inside or outside?
- ❑ Is it daytime or nighttime?
- ❑ What can the main character see?
- ❑ What can the main character hear?
- ❑ Is the place happy, scary, or peaceful?
- ❑ In what season does the story occur? How do you know?
- ❑ Is there anything unusual in the setting?

After answering these and other questions, have the child make a setting diorama and write a summary of the story.

Shoebox Diorama

For a shoebox diorama, cut one of the long sides off of a shoebox. Cut out and glue construction-paper objects to create the story setting. Use salt dough (page 124) or clay to create story characters or objects to include in the diorama.

Three-Sided Diorama

To make a three-sided diorama, begin with a 9" (23 cm) square of construction paper. Fold and crease the square diagonally. Then unfold it and fold and crease in the square on the opposite diagonal. Cut on one of the folded lines to the center. Completely overlap the two cut sections and glue them into place to form the diorama stage. Cut and glue setting objects to the background. Create stand-up objects by folding a tab at the base of cut objects and gluing them to the floor of the diorama.

Book Report Block

Fold the pattern on the dotted lines. Fill out the cube with the following information.

Box 1—Title of the book and author	**Box 4**—Where does the story take place?
Box 2—Who is the main character?	**Box 5**—What is your favorite part?
Box 3—What is the story about?	**Box 6**—Would you recommend the book?

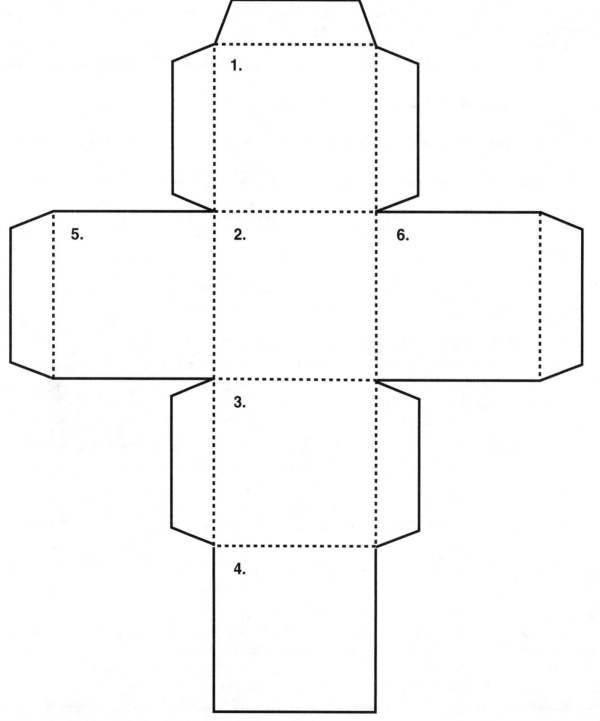

Story Picture Frame

Here's a great way for your students to write about and illustrate the events of a story. After selecting and reading a book, provide each child with a copy of the multi-picture story frame on page 78. The child cuts on the dotted lines to make the frame openings. Then the child glues the frame atop another sheet of colored printer paper or construction paper. The child begins by writing the book's title and author on the lines provided. In each of the openings, the child draws a picture of an event or character from the story. Below each picture, the child briefly writes to tell about the picture. Display each child's completed frame on a bulletin board entitled, "An Album of Stories."

 Standards and Benchmarks: 1G, 1H

Story Menus

This is a great project to accompany book reports about stories with food topics. Begin by having each child read or listen to one of the books below. Then have each child create a menu that would accompany the story. For example, in the book *Gregory, the Terrible Eater* by Mitchell Sharmot, Gregory the goat likes to eat "people food," such as fruits, vegetables, and spaghetti. His parents like to eat things like tin cans, paper, and shoelaces. By the end of the story, Gregory learns to appreciate both kinds of foods. After the story, a child might make a menu that looks like this:

Books about Food and Eating

- *Cloudy with a Chance of Meatballs* by Judy Barrett
- *Strega Nona* by Tomie dePaola
- *The Very Hungry Caterpillar* by Eric Carle
- *How My Parents Learned to Eat* by Ina R. Friedman
- *I Know an Old Lady Who Swallowed a Fly* by Nadine Westcott

---

Story Picture Frame

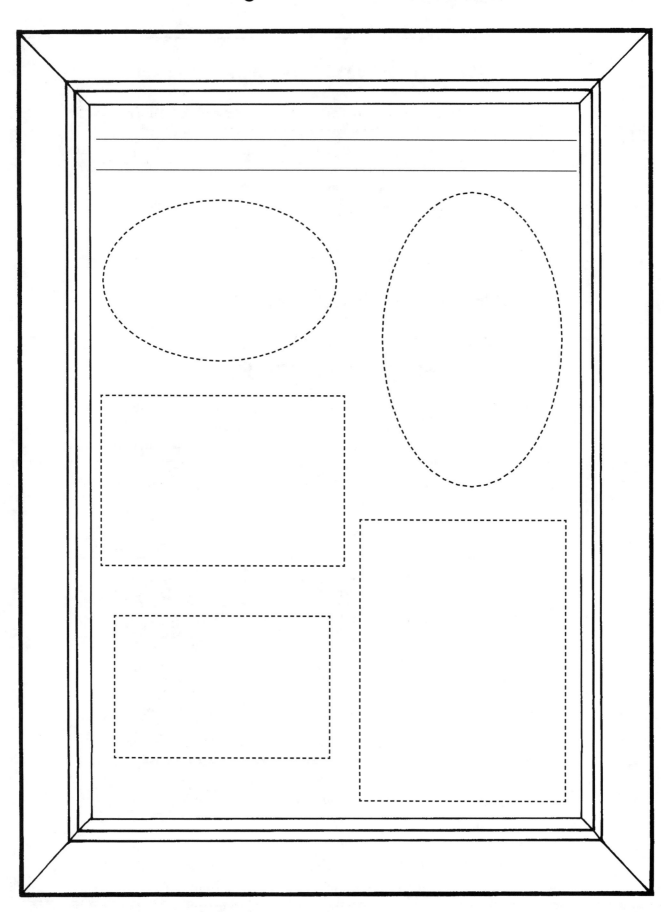

Visuals for Narratives

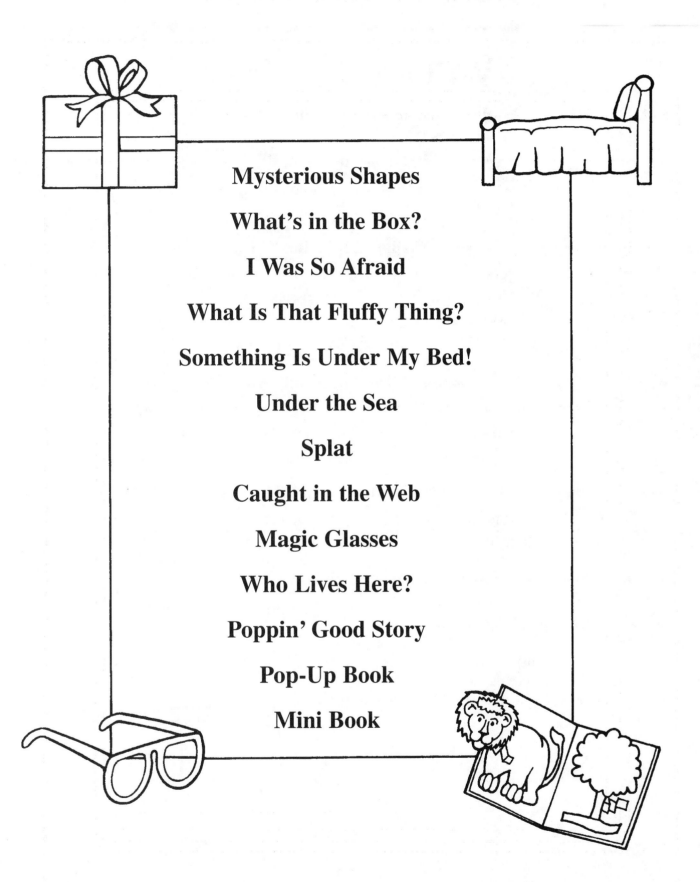

Mysterious Shapes

What's in the Box?

I Was So Afraid

What Is That Fluffy Thing?

Something Is Under My Bed!

Under the Sea

Splat

Caught in the Web

Magic Glasses

Who Lives Here?

Poppin' Good Story

Pop-Up Book

Mini Book

Writing Narratives

Spark your children's creativity with the projects in this section of the book.

"Mysterious Shapes"

- copy of pages 82 and 83
- pencil
- scissors
- crayons

"What's in the Box?"

- copy of page 84
- glue
- tissue paper
- ribbon
- crayons and/or markers
- scissors
- construction paper

"I Was So Afraid"

- copy of page 85
- scissors
- glue
- 9" x 13" (22.8 cm x 32.9 cm) sheet of construction paper
- crayons or markers

"What Is That Fluffy Thing?"

- copy of page 86
- glue
- cotton ball
- pencil or crayon

"Something Is Under My Bed!"

- copy of page 87
- scissors
- fabric or construction paper

Cut the fabric so that the bedspread covers the bed and the picture below it. Glue the bedspread to the bed only. Be sure not to glue it to the mystery picture.

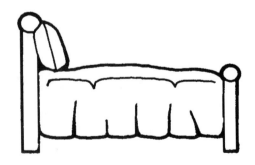

Writing Narratives *(cont.)*

"Under the Sea"

- copy of page 88
- newspaper
- waxed paper
- colored markers
- crayon shavings
- iron

Place the picture on several sheets of newspaper. Sprinkle crayon shavings over the picture. Place a piece of waxed paper over the picture. Use a warm iron atop the waxed paper to melt the crayon shavings and adhere the waxed paper to the picture.

"Splat"

- copy of page 89
- tempera paint
- newspaper
- paintbrushes

Spread newspaper over a large floor area. (You may even want to go outside for this one.) Lay a copy of page 89 atop the newspaper and then splatter one or more colors of tempera paint on the paper. Allow the paint to dry. Discuss with your children what a splatter picture might be, such as a squished bug, lunch dropped on the ground, an accident in art class, etc.

"Caught in the Web"

- copy of page 90
- scissors
- construction paper (assorted colors)
- colored yarn
- glue
- crayons or markers

"Magic Glasses"

- copy of page 91
- markers
- scissors
- crayons
- construction paper
- glue

"Who Lives Here?"

- copy of page 92
- black construction paper
- glue
- crayon markers
- scissors
- silver glitter

"Poppin' Good Story"

- copy of page 93
- glue
- two or three pieces of popped popcorn
- crayon or markers

Mysterious Shapes

Cut out one or two shapes from page 83. Trace them in the box below. Make each shape into a person, an animal, or an object. Color the picture. Below the box, write about the picture.

Mysterious Shapes *(cont.)*

What's in the Box?

Imagine that you are walking through a park. You find a pretty, wrapped box. There is a note on the box. What does it say? On the lines below, write a story about finding the box and what is inside. Decorate the box when you are finished.

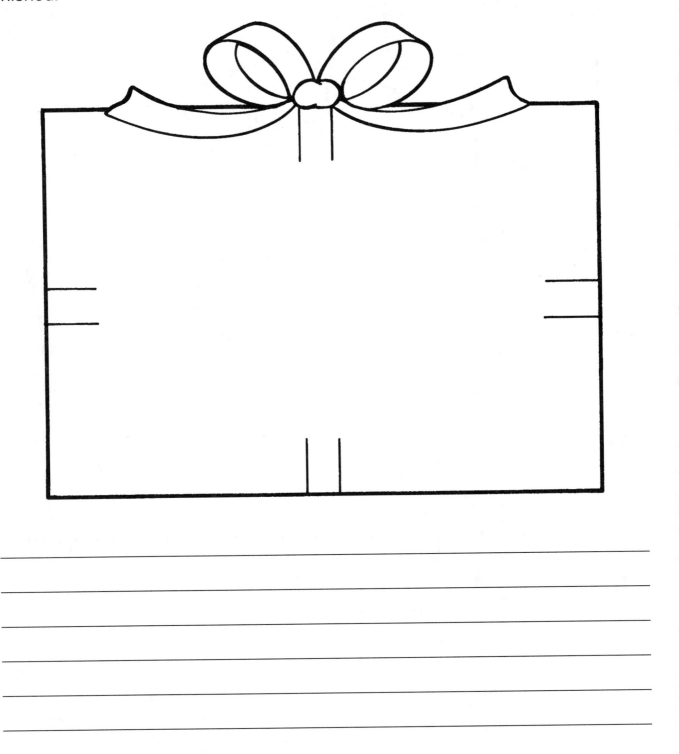

_____

_____

_____

_____

_____

_____

_____

I Was So Afraid

Imagine that you pass by an old house. You hear spooky noises. What's in the house? Would you go inside? On the lines below, write a story about the creepy house. Cut on the dotted lines to make door and window openings. Glue the paper to a sheet of construction paper. Color the picture and draw creatures behind the window shutters and door.

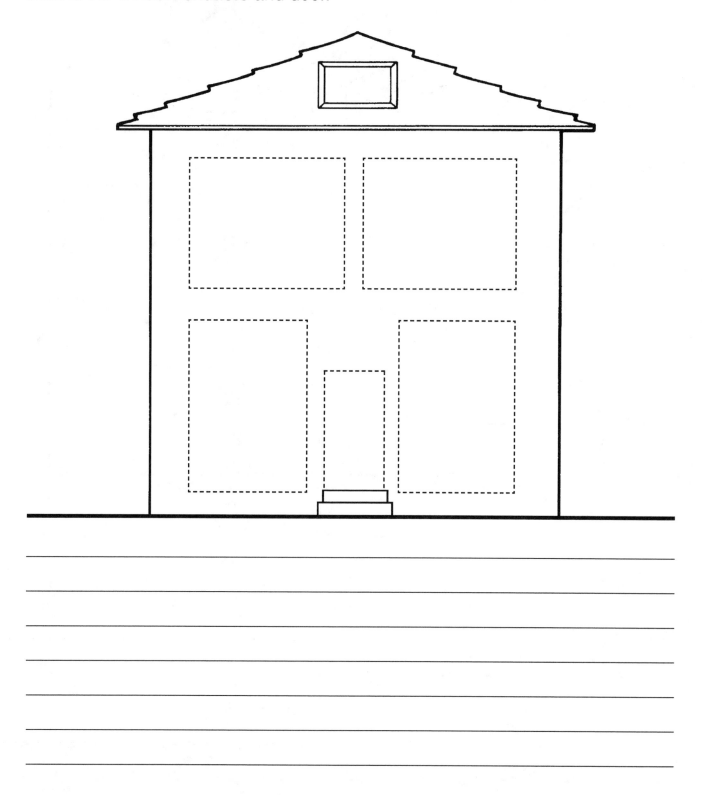

_____

_____

_____

_____

_____

_____

What Is That Fluffy Thing?

Glue a cotton ball in the frame below. Use a pencil or crayons to make it into a creature or an object. On the lines below, write a story about your creation.

_____

_____

_____

_____

_____

_____

Something Is Under My Bed!

Color a picture of something under the bed below. Make a bedspread out of colored construction paper or fabric. Glue the bedspread to the top of the bed. (Be sure not to glue it to the picture.) Write a mystery story about something under the bed. Invite your readers to guess what it might be. Then have them lift the bedspread to see.

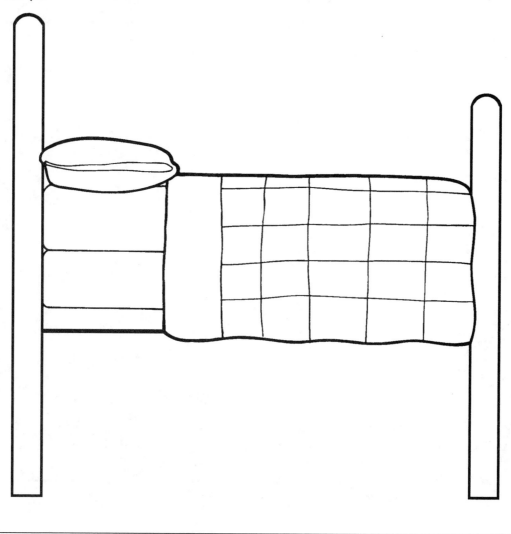

_____

_____

_____

_____

_____

_____

_____

Under the Sea

In the box below, use markers to draw a picture of yourself swimming in the ocean. Sprinkle crayon shavings over the picture. Place a piece of waxed paper over the picture. With the help of an adult, press a warm iron over the waxed paper to melt the crayon shavings. Write a story about your underwater adventure.

_____

_____

_____

_____

_____

_____

_____

Splat

What in the world is that? Use crayons, markers, or paint to add to your splatter picture. Write a story telling about what the splatter used to be and what happened to it.

_____

_____

_____

_____

_____

_____

_____

Caught in the Web

Glue pieces of colored yarn to the web below. Draw a spider on construction paper, cut it out, and glue it onto the web. Then imagine that a creature gets caught in the web. Draw and cut out a creature and glue it onto the web. Write a story about a friendship that begins between the spider and the creature.

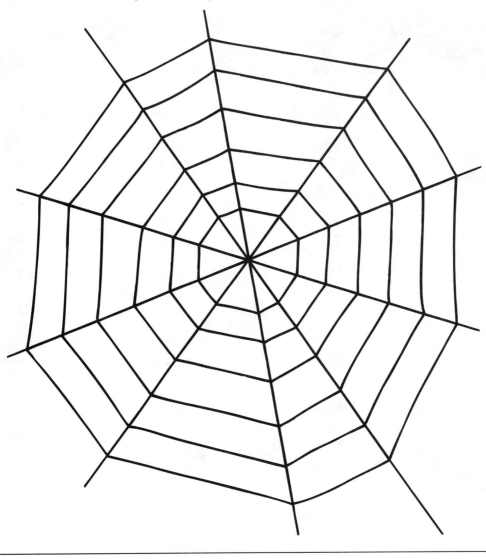

_____

_____

_____

_____

_____

_____

_____

Magic Glasses

The glasses you see below are magic. Use crayons, markers, construction paper, and glue to decorate them. Write a story telling about what happens when you put the glasses on. What can be seen? What can you do when you wear them? Paste your story onto a piece of construction paper and decorate it.

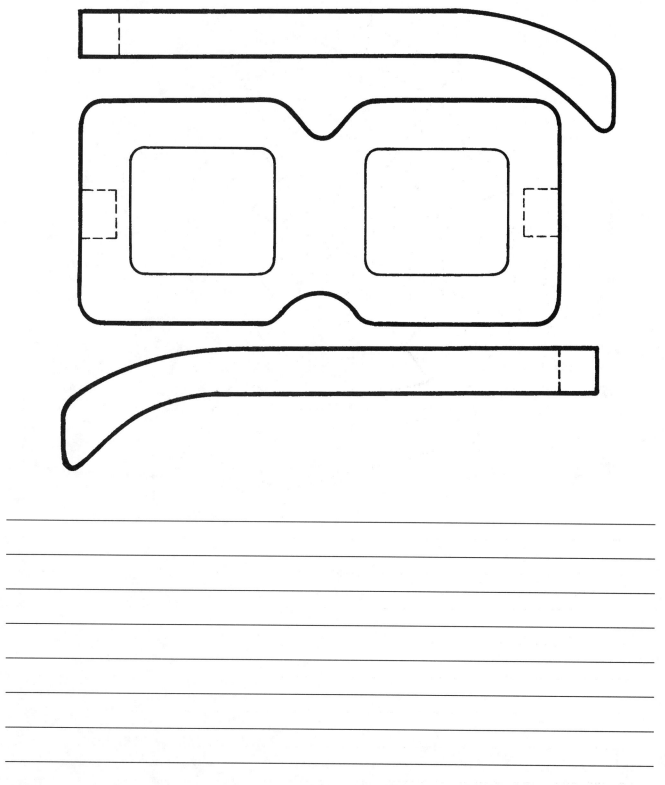

_____

_____

_____

_____

_____

_____

_____

_____

Who Lives Here?

What kinds of things live in caves? Draw a picture of a creature in the cave below. Cut out the cave and glue it to black construction paper. Squeeze dots of glue on the black paper. Sprinkle silver glitter on the glue to make stars. Shake off the excess glitter. Write a story about your cave creature and staple it to the picture.

_____

_____

_____

_____

_____

_____

_____

Poppin' Good Story

Glue two or three pieces of popcorn in the box below. What could they be? Could they be the tops of flowers or scoops of ice cream? Could they be hats or hair or animals? Use a pencil or crayons to add details. Write a story about your picture.

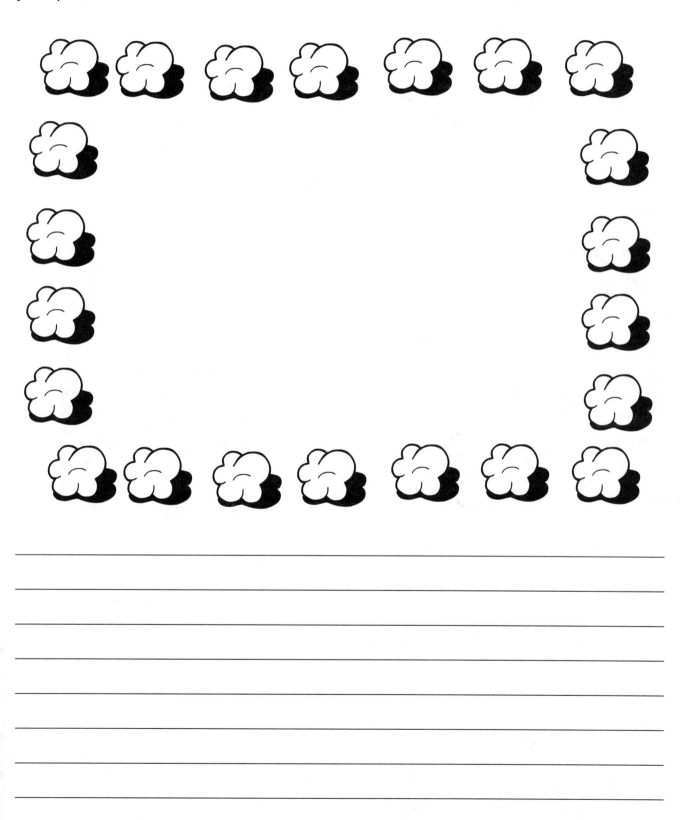

_____

_____

_____

_____

_____

_____

Pop-Up Book

Your children can creatively publish their stories by making pop-up books.

Materials

- several sheets of 9" x 13" (22.8 cm x 32.9 cm) construction paper
- scissors
- glue
- white construction paper
- markers, crayons, or colored pencils

Directions

1. Fold the sheets of colored construction paper in half lengthwise; crease the foldlines. Working with one sheet at a time, cut two slits just off center so that the total width of the cut portion equals one or two inches (2.5 or 5 cm).

2. Halfway open one sheet. Using your index finger, "pop" forward the cut section. Refold the sheet and crease the foldlines once again; reopen the sheet and set aside. Repeat this process with the remaining sheets.

3. Have the child write a portion of the story on each page. The child then uses white construction paper to color, cut out, and glue a matching illustration to the pop-up portion of the page.

4. When all the pages have been completed, glue the top half of the first page to the bottom half of the second page. Then glue the top half of the second page to the bottom half of the third page. Continue this process until all of the pages have been glued together. (Note: Be careful not to glue down the pop-up portion of each page.)

5. Create a cover for the book by gluing on a half-sheet of colored construction paper to the front of the book. Title the book and decorate.

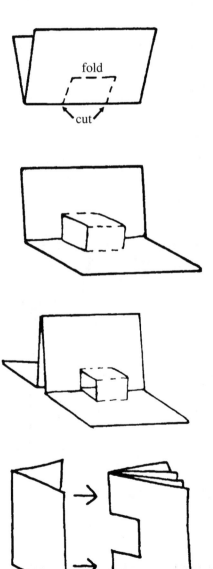

Mini Book

Follow these steps below to make small books to display children's narratives.

How to Make a Mini Book

Step 1: Hold the paper tall. Fold down, then across, then down again.

Step 2: Open the paper to the first fold. Cut halfway down the horizontal fold.

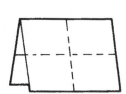

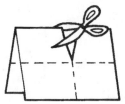

Step 3: Open the paper. Refold so the opening is at the top. Push the two edges together so the cut pages form a square.

Step 4: Continue pushing to close the gap. Fold all the pages to form an eight-page booklet (including front and back cover).

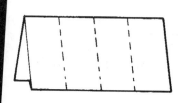

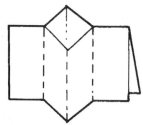

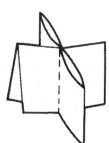

Visuals for Topics

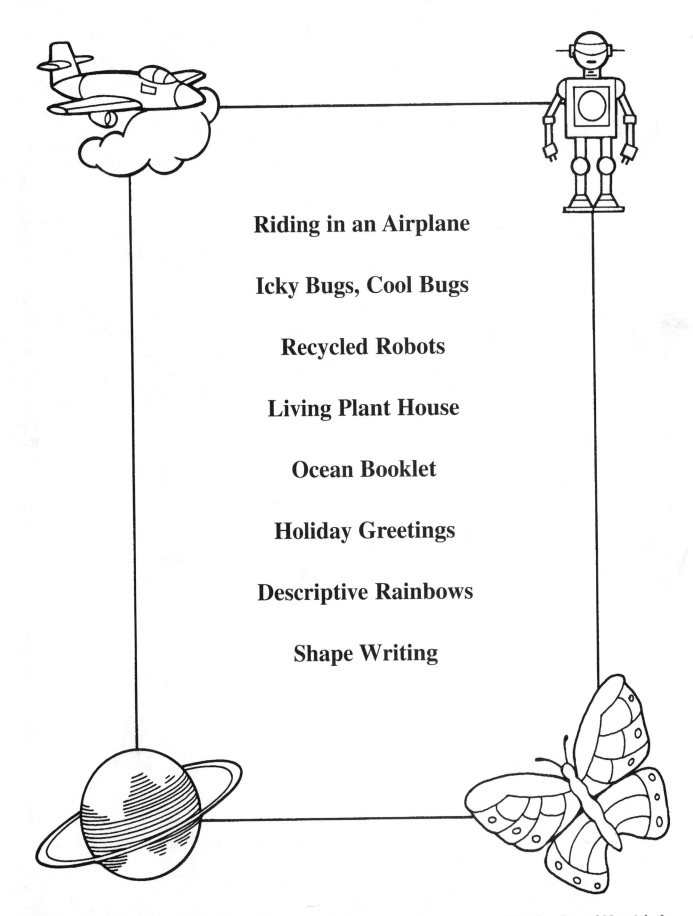

Riding in an Airplane

Icky Bugs, Cool Bugs

Recycled Robots

Living Plant House

Ocean Booklet

Holiday Greetings

Descriptive Rainbows

Shape Writing

Visual Activities

Riding in an Airplane

Have your children think about what it would be like to ride in an airplane. Allow children to share their experiences on airplanes. Show them photographs of airplanes and allow the children to respond to them. After students write about riding in an airplane (page 98), show them how to make a paper airplane (see instructions on page 99). (**Note:** To further explore the topic, read *Angela's Airplane* by Robert Munsch with the class.)

Icky Bugs, Cool Bugs

Share books with your students about insects and spiders. Engage the children in a discussion about bugs. Do they like them? Do they think bugs are creepy? Distribute copies of the writing frame on page 100 and have the children write about their experiences with bugs. Then show them how to make egg carton bugs (page 101).

Suggested Bug Books

Icky Bug Counting Book by Jerry Pallotta

Miss Spider's Tea Party by David Kirk

Alpha Bugs: A Pop-Up Alphabet by David A. Carter

Recycled Robots

Wouldn't it be great to have a robot? What kinds of things could a robot do for you? Distribute copies of page 102 and have the children write about robots. Then have them make three-dimensional robots to accompany their writing.

Living Plant House

Growing plants can be exciting. This activity allows your children to grow plants, write about them, and create decorative displays. See page 104 for instructions.

Riding in an Airplane

Flying in an airplane can be exciting or scary. Think about what it would be like to ride in an airplane. Tell a story about this experience. Write your story below.

When you are finished, make a paper airplane.

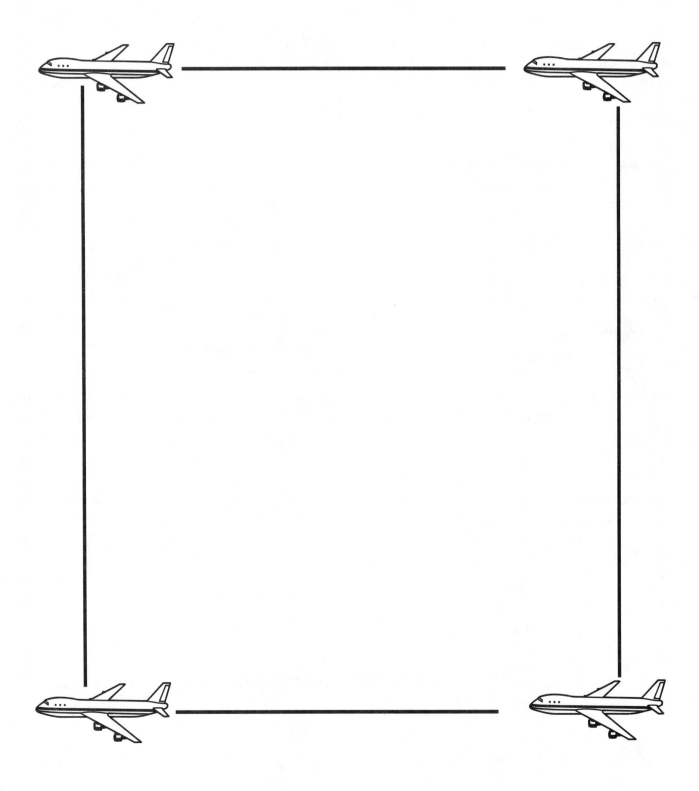

Making a Paper Airplane

Use the instructions below to assist in demonstrating how to make a paper airplane.

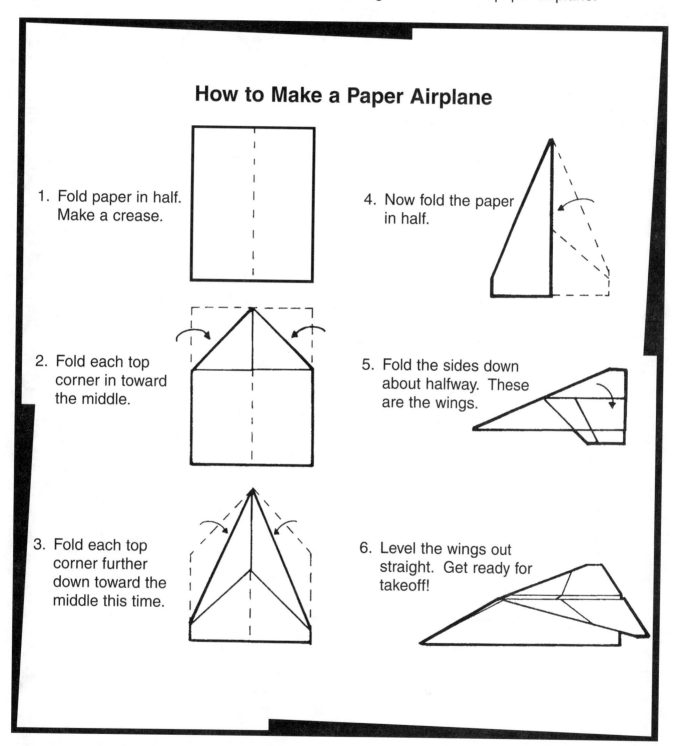

How to Make a Paper Airplane

1. Fold paper in half. Make a crease.

2. Fold each top corner in toward the middle.

3. Fold each top corner further down toward the middle this time.

4. Now fold the paper in half.

5. Fold the sides down about halfway. These are the wings.

6. Level the wings out straight. Get ready for takeoff!

Icky Bugs, Cool Bugs

I think bugs are _____

_____

My favorite bug is _____

_____

because _____

_____

The bug I hate the most is _____

because _____

_____

_____

One time I saw a bug and _____

_____

_____

_____

_____

_____

_____

_____

Egg-Carton Bugs

Materials

- paper egg cartons
- thick tempera paint (desired colors)
- paintbrush
- scissors
- construction-paper scraps (assorted colors)
- hole puncher
- glue
- pipe cleaners

Directions

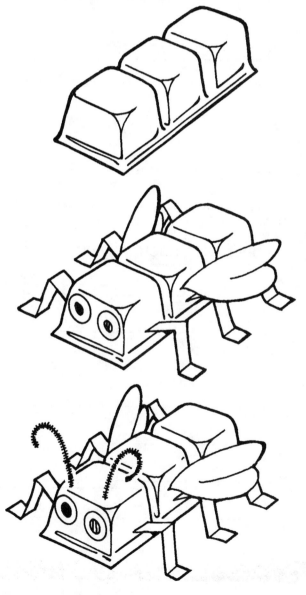

1. Cut a one-, two-, or three-segment piece of egg carton for a bug.

2. Paint the egg carton with thick tempera paint and allow it to dry.

3. Cut out legs and wings from construction paper and glue them onto the egg carton.

4. Cut two half-inch (1.25 cm) circles for eyes and glue them to the head of the bug. Use a hole puncher to punch two circles (each a different color) and glue them to the center of the eyes.

5. Cut two 2-inch (5 cm) pieces of pipe cleaner for antennae (for an insect). Press the pipe cleaner pieces into the top of the first segment and curl the ends.

If I Had a Robot

If I had a robot, its name would be _____

My robot would be able to do _____

_____

_____

_____

In the morning, my robot would _____

_____

_____

At night, my robot would _____

_____

_____

The best thing about having a robot would be _____

_____

_____

_____

_____

_____

_____

Making Recycled Robots

Materials

- glue
- scissors
- markers
- tape
- construction paper
- an assortment of the following items
    - milk jugs
    - two-liter plastic bottles
    - boxes
    - buttons
    - tissue-paper rolls
    - egg cartons

Directions

1. To make a robot, choose a large item such as a milk jug or a two-liter plastic bottle to use for the body.

2. Glue or tape on smaller items to make facial features, arms, legs, and other robot details.

3. Add other parts to the robot by cutting and gluing on construction-paper shapes.

4. Write the robot's name on a name tag and attach it to the robot's body.

Living Plant House

Materials

- plastic sandwich bag
- 4" x 4" (10 cm x 10 cm) piece of paper towel
- stapler and staples
- bird seed
- water
- living plant house pattern (page 105)
- scissors
- crayons
- pencil
- *The Tiny Seed* by Eric Carle

Directions

1. Slide the paper towel into the plastic bag.

2. Make a row of staples one inch (2.5 cm) from the bottom of the bag.

3. Sprinkle five or six bird seeds into the bag. (They should rest on the staples.)

4. Slowly pour water into the bag, allowing it to fill the section below the staple line.

5. Staple the top of the bag to a wall display.

6. Next, cut out the plant house pattern on the bold lines. Cut on the dotted lines to cut out the center of the house.

7. Decorate the house using crayons. Then, on this line, write about what plants need in order to grow on the lines.

8. Staple the completed house atop the plastic bag so that the bag shows in the cutout window. Be sure not to staple the top of the bag closed, so water can be added, as needed.

Living Plant House *(cont.)*

Ocean Booklet

Ocean animals are fascinating to children, and this booklet helps to creatively display your children's research. Have each child select an ocean animal to research. Allow the children to obtain children's nonfiction books from the school or local library. Teach the children how to gather information by writing facts in their own words. Have them keep their gathered facts on note cards or small sheets of paper. When all the information is collected, have each child create an ocean waves booklet for his or her written work.

Materials

- ocean waves booklet pages (pages 107 and 108)
- blue copier paper (in varying shades)
- pencil
- scissors
- stapler
- crayons

Directions

1. Cut out the booklet pages and trace each onto blue copier paper.

2. Cut out the pages and stack them in a graduated format (as shown).

3. Staple the booklet along the bottom edge of the booklet.

4. Write a title for the report on the cover of the booklet.

5. On each of the booklet pages, write research information and color an accompanying illustration.

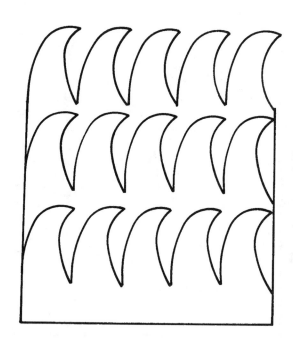

Ocean Booklet Pages

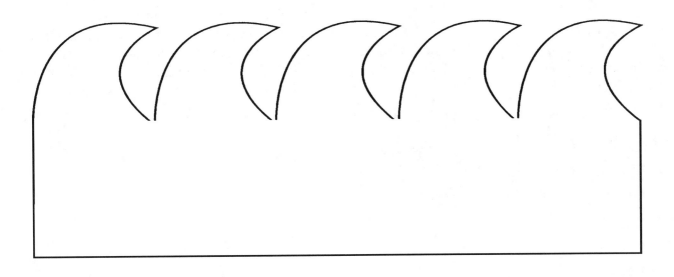

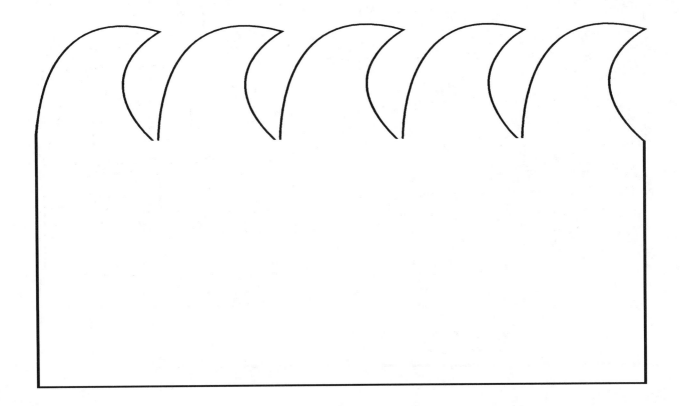

Ocean Booklet Pages *(cont.)*

Holiday Greetings

This writing project can be used to create cards for holidays or any occasion.

Materials

- small cups
- water
- food coloring
- 4" x 6" (10 cm x 15.2 cm) sheets of paper towel
- pencil
- 9" x 13" (22.8 cm x 32.9 cm) sheet of construction paper
- scissors
- glue

Directions

1. In each of several cups, mix water and a different color of food coloring.

2. Fold the paper towel in half and then fold it in half again.

3. Dip each corner of the folded paper towel in a different cup and allow the colored water to be absorbed.

4. Squeeze out the excess water, unfold the paper towel, and allow it to dry.

5. Fold the construction paper in half two times to make a card.

6. Draw a holiday shape (Christmas tree, dreidel, Easter bunny, etc.).

7. Glue the dried paper towel behind the cutout to make a colorful holiday card.

8. Inside the card, have the child write a greeting to a friend or loved one.

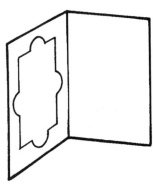

Descriptive Rainbows

Give your students the opportunity to write descriptively with this attractive project.

Materials

- rainbow pattern (page 111)
- colored pencils or fine tip markers (assorted colors)
- glue
- tagboard
- scissors
- crepe-paper streamers (assorted colors)
- hole puncher
- yarn
- *Hailstones and Halibut Bones* by Mary O'Neil

Directions

1. Have a discussion with your children about rainbows. Have they ever seen one? How could a rainbow be described?

2. Brainstorm a list of words describing rainbows and write them on chart paper. See the list below for suggestions.

Rainbow Words

• red	• yellow
• blue	• purple
• colorful	• misty
• beautiful	• decorative
• peaceful	• huge
• lucky	• mysterious

---

3. Provide each child with a copy of the rainbow pattern. Have each child use a pencil or marker of a contrasting color to write descriptive words on each band of the rainbow.

4. Glue the rainbow to a sheet of tagboard and then cut it out.

5. Glue different colored crepe-paper streamers along the base of the rainbow.

6. Punch a hole in the top of the rainbow and tie a loop of yarn through it for suspending.

Descriptive Rainbow Pattern

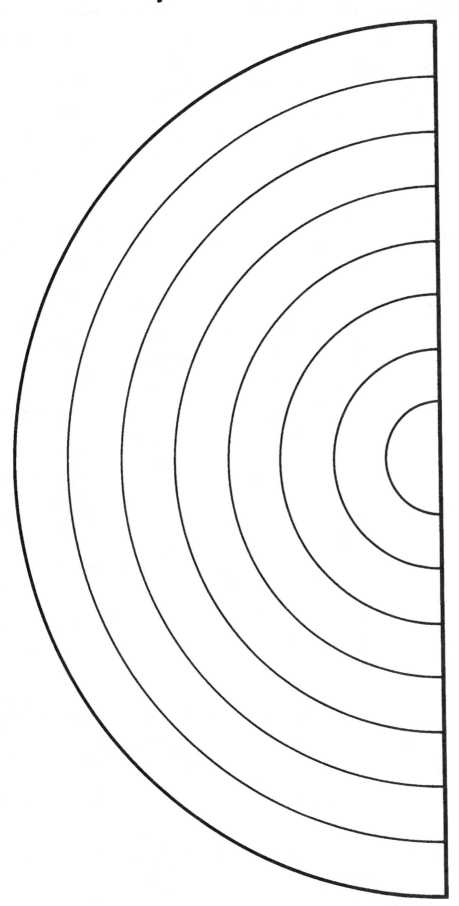

Shape Writing

Pages 113–119 are reproducibles designed to inspire your children's writing on a variety of topics. Refer to the following suggestions for use with each shape-writing page.

Fall Leaf

- ❏ seasons
- ❏ colors of trees
- ❏ animals that live in trees

- ❏ change
- ❏ fall holidays or celebrations
- ❏ Thanksgiving or Halloween party invitation

Snowman

- ❏ winter
- ❏ snow
- ❏ outdoor winter activities

- ❏ building a snowman
- ❏ weather
- ❏ winter holidays or celebrations

Flower

- ❏ spring
- ❏ planting seeds
- ❏ plant life cycle

- ❏ caring for flowers
- ❏ Mother's Day

Sun

- ❏ weather
- ❏ summertime
- ❏ outdoor activities

- ❏ picnics
- ❏ end-of-the-year party invitation

Monster

- ❏ things that are scary
- ❏ a scary adventure

- ❏ Halloween

Shoe

- ❏ sports
- ❏ going places

- ❏ favorite shoes

Bus

- ❏ field trip
- ❏ school

- ❏ going on a trip
- ❏ favorite school events

Shape Writing *(cont.)*

Fall Leaf

Shape Writing *(cont.)*
Snowman

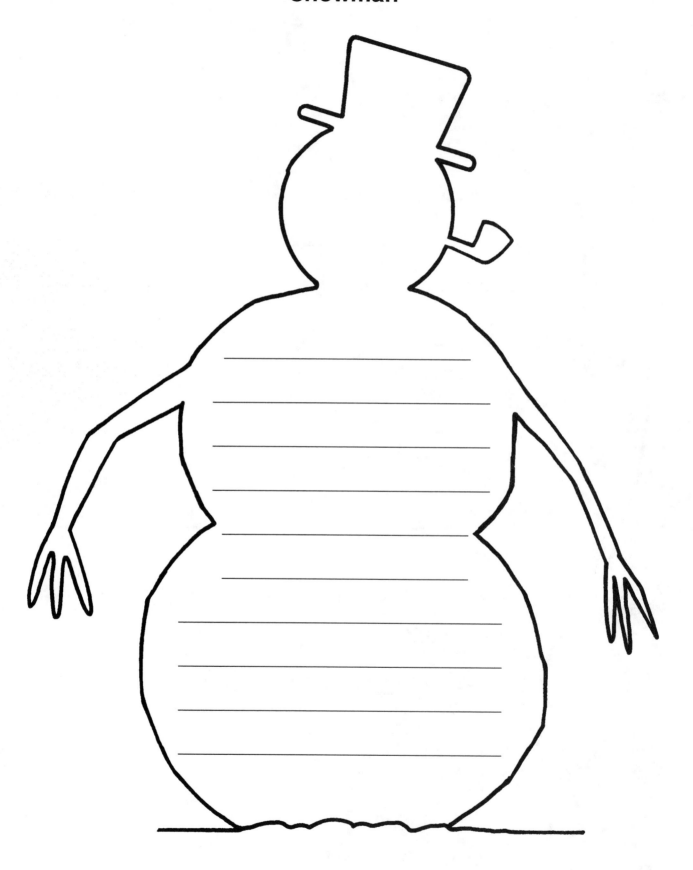

Shape Writing *(cont.)*
Flower

Shape Writing *(cont.)*
Sun

Shape Writing *(cont.)*
Monster

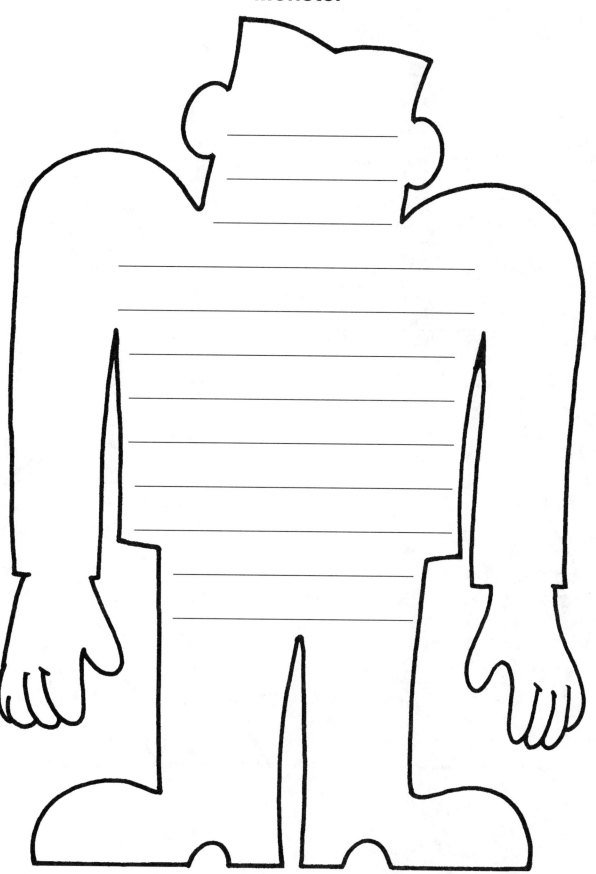

Shape Writing *(cont.)*
Shoe

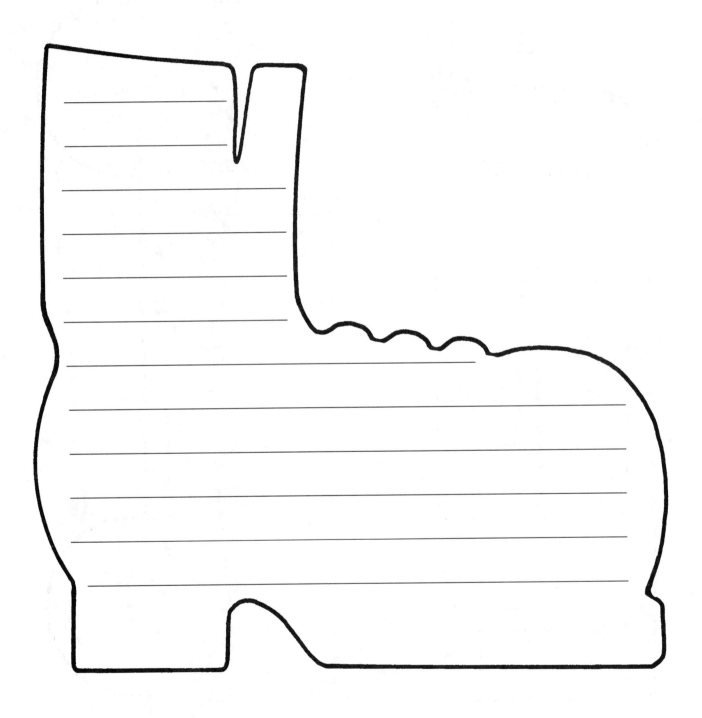

Shape Writing *(cont.)*

Bus

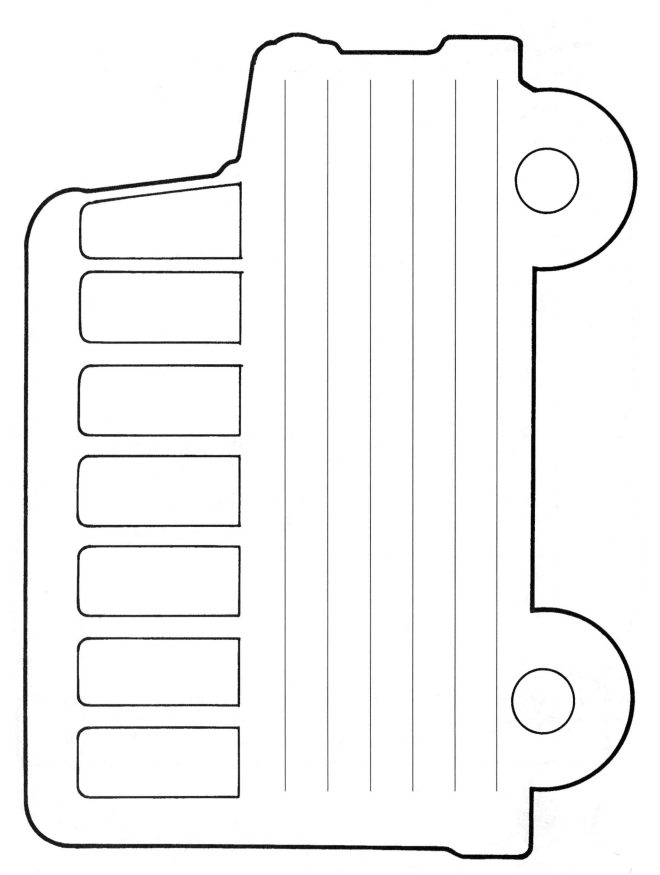

More Visual-Aid Projects

Paints, Dough, and Techniques

Stencils

Class Scrapbooks

Individual Portfolios

Planning a Presentation

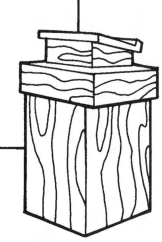

Paints, Dough, and Techniques

Have your children try these fun and creative techniques to make eye-catching illustrations to accompany their edited written work.

Decorative Dye

Materials

- seeds, rice, pasta, or dried flowers
- small container with a lid
- rubbing alcohol
- food coloring
- paper towels
- glue
- construction paper or tagboard

Directions

Color seeds, rice, pasta, and dried flowers with this easy dye recipe. In a small, lidded container, place one tablespoon of rubbing alcohol and six drops of food coloring. Swirl gently to mix. Place the objects to be dyed into the mixture and secure the lid. Shake the container gently for a minute or two. Spread the dyed objects on sheets of paper towel to dry. Then glue the objects to construction paper or tagboard to create a design.

Milky Paint

This paint gives illustrations a creamy look.

Materials

- evaporated milk
- food coloring
- plastic containers
- spoons
- paintbrushes
- construction paper

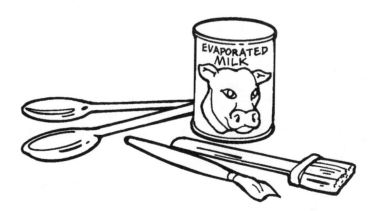

Directions

Place evaporated milk into the containers. Add a different color of food coloring to each container. Mix and continue adding food coloring until the desired color is achieved. Paint pictures on construction paper.

Paints, Dough, and Techniques *(cont.)*

Crystallized Paint

As this paint dries, colored crystals will form.

Materials

- two cups of water
- two cups of Epsom salt
- saucepan
- heating element
- spoon
- food coloring
- paintbrush
- construction paper

Directions

Place water and Epsom salt in the saucepan and bring to a boil. Allow the mixture to cool. Add food coloring and mix. Paint an illustration onto white construction paper.

See-Through Paint

This recipe results in a transparent paint that gives an unusual appearance to art work.

Materials

- pencils
- construction paper
- light corn syrup
- small plastic containers
- food coloring
- spoons
- paintbrushes

Directions

On a sheet of construction paper, draw the outline only of the desired illustration. Mix corn syrup and a different color of food coloring in each of the plastic containers. Use the paintbrushes to paint within the outline of the illustration. Allow several days for the picture to dry.

Paints, Dough, and Techniques *(cont.)*

Colored Glue

Colored glue makes interesting pictures with a raised textured look.

Materials

- crayons, tempera paint, or watercolors
- construction paper
- tempera paint (assorted colors)
- small school glue bottles (partially filled)

Directions

Color or paint a picture on construction paper. Then mix school glue and different colors of tempera paint in each of several glue bottles. Mix to create the desired color. (Do not add too much tempera or the glue will be too thin.) Squeeze the desired color of glue along the edges of painted or colored objects on the picture to outline. Allow the glue to dry while laying flat.

Glitter Pictures

Make dazzling illustrations with this technique.

Materials

- newspaper
- dark-colored construction paper
- pencil
- glue
- glitter (assorted colors)

Directions

Cover a flat surface with newspaper. On the construction paper, draw a simple outline (as large as possible) of the desired illustration. Squeeze a trail of glue along a portion of the outline and sprinkle it with the desired color of glitter. Shake off the excess. Continue in this manner, apply glue and glitter until the entire outline is covered. Allow the finished product to dry completely before displaying.

Paints, Dough, and Techniques *(cont.)*

Salt Dough

Salt dough can be used to make story characters, three-dimensional maps, and a variety of other visual aids to accompany writing.

Materials

- 1 cup of salt
- 2 cups of flour
- 1 cup of water

Directions

Mix all three ingredients together until a pliable dough forms. If the mixture is sticky, add a bit more flour. If the mixture is too dry, add a bit more water. Allow the dough creations to dry for several days before painting with tempera paint.

Newspaper Dough

This dough results in projects that are sturdy and easily painted.

Materials

- large mixing bowl
- newspaper strips
- water
- flour

Directions

In the bowl, place a large quantity of newspaper strips. Cover the strips completely with water and allow to stand overnight. The next day, pour out the water and squeeze out the excess from the newspaper. Mix flour and water to make a wet pasty mixture and add to the newspaper. Knead the paste and newspaper until a soft, gray dough is formed. (Add more paste as needed.) Allow the dough creations to dry for several days before painting with tempera paint.

Coffee Dough

This dough looks like natural rock when dry and can be used to make a variety of items, such as beads, medallions and geographic rock formations.

Materials

- 1 cup of salt
- 2 cups of flour
- 1 cup of water
- ⅛ cup of dried (used) coffee grounds

Directions

Mix the ingredients together and knead to create a pliable, speckled dough. If the mixture is sticky, add a bit more flour. If the mixture is too dry, add a bit more water. Allow dough creations to dry for several days. (If making beads or medallions, be sure to make holes for stringing when the dough is still soft.) Painting is not necessary.

Stencils

Sponge Stencils

With this technique, your children can create simple illustrations to accompany their written work.

Materials

- stencils (cut from construction paper or copied and cut from pages 126 and 127)
- tape
- white construction paper
- tempera paint (selected colors)
- small plastic bowls
- 2-inch sponge squares or crumpled paper towels

Directions

Use rolls of tape to temporarily attach the stencils to the white construction paper. Place the desired colors of paint in the bowls. Dip sponges or crumpled paper towels into the paint and then press onto the paper. (Several colors may be overlapped.) Use this sponge-painting technique to cover the entire paper (including the stencils). Remove and discard the stencils and tape, revealing the finished project.

Splatter Stencils

Materials

- stencils (cut from construction paper or copied and cut from pages 126 and 127)
- tape
- white construction paper
- art smock
- water
- food coloring
- small containers
- colander
- toothbrush

Directions

Temporarily attach the stencils to the white construction paper using rolls of tape. Mix water and different colors of food coloring in the small containers. (Be sure to wear an art smock or other covering to protect clothing.) Place the colander atop the stencil. Dip the toothbrush into the colored mixture and then brush it on the colander. Color will splatter onto the paper below. Continue in this manner using different colors until the desired coverage is achieved. Remove the colander, stencils, and tape to reveal the finished product.

Stencils *(cont.)*

Stencils *(cont.)*

Standards and Benchmarks: 1H, 3B

Class Scrapbooks

Scrapbooks are great ways to display memories from field trips, special events, or even to document the happenings of a school year. Get your children involved in making an album of memories.

Materials

- three-ring binder
- three-hole punch
- assorted memorabilia, such as . . .

    —photographs
    —student work

- construction paper
- glue

    —brochures
    —student-made illustrations

Directions

1. Determine the type of scrapbook to be made, such as a field-trip scrapbook or a yearbook of memories. Ask the children to think of things that might be collected to add to the scrapbook.
2. Assemble the scrapbook by three-hole punching sheets of construction paper and placing them in the binder.
3. During the field trip or throughout the year, have the children collect memorable items for the scrapbook.
4. When an item is added to the scrapbook, the child writes a few sentences telling about it.
5. Display the scrapbook at Open House or conferences for parents to enjoy.

Standards and Benchmarks: 1H, 3B

Individual Portfolios

Materials

- three-ring binder
- three-hole punch
- copies of page 129

- construction paper
- selected student work

- glue or stapler
- scissors

Directions

1. Three-hole punch the construction paper sheets and put them in a binder for each child.
2. Have each child select class work to glue or staple in the binder. The child should select work that shows his or her progress throughout the year.
3. After placing an item in the portfolio, the child cuts a strip from page 129 and writes about the selected work. Then he or she attaches the strip to the bottom of the portfolio page.

Portfolio Strips

I chose this work because _____

_____

This work shows that I learned _____

_____

_____

I chose this work because _____

_____

This work shows that I learned _____

_____

_____

I chose this work because _____

_____

This work shows that I learned _____

_____

_____

I chose this work because _____

_____

_____

This work shows that I learned _____

_____

Planning a Presentation

Hello. My name is _____

My presentation is about _____

Here are some important things you should know about _____

_____

_____

_____

_____

_____

_____

This is the visual project I made. (Show the project.)

(Write the things you want to say about your project.)

_____

_____

_____

This topic was interesting because _____

_____

_____

Are there any questions?

Assessment

Using Rubrics

Writing Mechanics Rubric

Content and Organization Rubric

Visual Aids (General) Rubric

Maps and Diagrams Rubric

Charts and Graphs Rubric

Skills Checklist

Writing and Visuals Self-Assessment

Using Rubrics

Why Use a Rubric?

Using rubrics to assess student work helps you and your children identify quality work. Using rubrics to grade your children's writing and visual projects will save time and make the grading easier because each step of the four-point rubric describes the requirements needed in order to receive that score. This will help you convey to students and parents the areas of strengths and weaknesses in written assignments.

What Is a Four-point Rubric?

- ❑ A four-point rubric is a scale that represents different levels of writing. Each level outlines skills demonstrated in writing. You can find several rubrics on pages 134–138.

- ❑ A four-point response indicates that the child incorporates all the requirements for the assignment. A four-point score also indicates that very little improvement is needed.

- ❑ A three-point response indicates that the child incorporates most of the requirements for the assignment. There may be a few errors, but the writing or project is clear and has only a slight need for improvement.

- ❑ A two-point response indicates that the child exhibits many errors in the content of the assignment. The writing or project tends to be unclear and illogically sequenced. Significant revision is needed to improve the work.

- ❑ A one-point response indicates weak writing skills or quality of the project with the need for improvement in a variety of areas. This score often demonstrates the need for reteaching and careful revision.

How Do I Create My Own Rubric?

This book provides several rubrics to use for assessing your children's work. These include mechanics, content and organization, basic visual aids, maps and diagrams, and charts and graphs. However, you may find it is necessary to create your own rubric to meet the needs of your students and the specific lessons you teach. Use the following steps to create your own rubric:

1. Determine the goal of the assignment.

2. Select criteria for the highest performance of the assignment.

3. Determine whether you would like to create a three- or four-point rubric. Then write the criteria for the descending levels. Keep in mind that the one-point score usually involves the absence of most of the requirements of the assignment.

4. Use the frame on page 133 to create your rubric.

Using Rubrics *(cont.)*

Use this rubric frame to write your own writing assessment.

Scoring Rubric

4 Points

The child:

3 Points

The child:

2 Points

The child:

1 Point

The child:

Using Rubrics *(cont.)*

Writing Mechanics

4 Points

The child consistently spells high-frequency words correctly. Proper end marks and commas in a series are used. The child consistently capitalizes the first word of a sentence. The child capitalizes proper nouns. Sentences are complete and use proper noun/verb agreement.

3 Points

The child's writing is relatively free of spelling errors. Most of the sentences contain proper end marks and commas. Capital letters are used at the beginning of most sentences and proper nouns. The writing is grammatically correct and sentences are complete.

2 Points

The child's writing includes some spelling errors. The writing has inconsistent use of end marks and capitalization. The writing has some evidence of incomplete sentences.

1 Point

The child's swriting contains many spelling, punctuation, and capitalization errors. Incorrect grammar and incomplete sentences dominate the work.

Using Rubrics *(cont.)*

Content and Organization

4 Points

The piece is clearly written and contains a central purpose. The work contains descriptive words and details to make the writing interesting. All information is relevant to the purpose of the piece. Sentences are complete and written in logical sequence.

3 Points

The piece is clearly written and contains a fairly clear purpose. The work contains some descriptive words and details to make the writing interesting. Most of the information is relevant to the purpose of the piece. Most of the sentences are complete and written in logical sequence.

2 Points

The writing's purpose is somewhat unclear. Few descriptive words and details are used to make the piece interesting. Some irrelevant information is included. The writing contains some incomplete sentences and logical sequence is not always used.

1 Point

The purpose of the writing is unclear. The piece does not contain descriptive words or details. Irrelevant information is included. Most sentences are not complete and/or do not follow logical sequence.

Visual Aids (General)

4 Points

The project relates to the child's written work in a meaningful way. The project is finished and was neatly created. The child is able to clearly tell about the project and why he or she created it to enhance the written work.

3 Points

The project relates to the child's written work in a meaningful way. The project is finished and was neatly created. In a fairly clear manner, the child is able to tell about the project and why he or she created it to enhance the written work.

2 Points

The project relates to the child's written work in some way. The project may or may not be finished and neatly created. The child is able to tell about the project but may not be able to tell how it enhances the written work.

1 Point

The project does not clearly relate to the child's written work in a meaningful way. The project is messy and may not be finished. The child is not able to tell about the project and how it relates to the written work.

Using Rubrics *(cont.)*

Maps and Diagrams

4 Points

The map or diagram relates to the child's written work in a meaningful way. The project is finished and was neatly created. A diagram is properly titled and labeled. A map is properly labeled and includes a compass rose and key. The child is able to tell about the project and why he or she created it to enhance the written work.

3 Points

The map or diagram relates to the child's written work in a meaningful way. The project is finished and was neatly created. A diagram is properly titled and labeled. A map is properly labeled and includes a compass rose and key. The child is able to tell about the project but may not be able to make a meaningful connection with the written work.

2 Points

The map or diagram relates to the child's written work in some way. The project may or may not be finished and neatly created. A diagram may not have a title or all the needed labels. A map may not have all the necessary labels and the compass rose or key is omitted. The child may or may not be able to tell about the project and why he or she created it to enhance the written work.

1 Point

The map or diagram does not clearly relate to the child's written work in a meaningful way. The project is messy and may not be finished. Diagrams and maps do not have the necessary labels and components. The child is not able to clearly discuss the project and how it relates to the written work.

Using Rubrics *(cont.)*

Charts and Graphs

4 Points

The chart or graph relates to the child's written work in a meaningful way. The project is finished and was neatly created. The child correctly titles and labels the chart or graph. He or she is able to discuss the project and how it enhances the written work.

3 Points

The chart or graph relates to the child's written work in a meaningful way. The project is finished and was neatly created. The child has titled the project and most of the labeling is correct. He or she is able to discuss the project and how it enhances the written work.

2 Points

The chart or graph relates to the child's written work in some way. The project may or may not be neatly created. The child demonstrates difficulty with labeling and titling the chart or graph. He or she may or may not be able to discuss the project and how it enhances the written work.

1 Point

The chart or graph does not relate to the child's written work in a meaningful way. The project is not complete or has a messy appearance. The child has not titled or labeled the chart or graph. He or she is not able to discuss the project and how it enhances the written work.

Skills Checklist

Child's Name: _____

Prewriting
- ❏ discusses ideas with peers
- ❏ draws pictures to generate ideas

Drafting and Revising
- ❏ rereads
- ❏ rearranges words, sentences, paragraphs
- ❏ adds descriptive words and details
- ❏ incorporates suggestions from others

Editing and Publishing
- ❏ proofreads
- ❏ edits grammar, punctuation, spelling, etc.
- ❏ evaluates own and others' writing
- ❏ asks questions about writing
- ❏ makes comments about writing
- ❏ helps apply grammatical and mechanical conventions
- ❏ uses logical sequence
- ❏ includes beginning, middle, and end
- ❏ uses detailed descriptions
- ❏ describes people, places, and things
- ❏ writes in response to literature
- ❏ writes in a variety of formats

Skills Checklist *(cont.)*

Uses grammatical and mechanical conventions
- ❏ uses complete sentences
- ❏ uses declarative sentences
- ❏ uses interrogative sentences
- ❏ uses nouns
- ❏ uses verbs
- ❏ uses adjectives
- ❏ uses adverbs
- ❏ uses proper spelling
- ❏ uses resources to spell correctly
- ❏ capitalizes beginning of sentences
- ❏ capitalizes proper nouns
- ❏ uses proper end marks
- ❏ uses commas in a series

Gathers and uses information for research purposes
- ❏ generates questions about topics of interest
- ❏ uses books to gather information for research topics

Comments:_____

_____

_____

_____

_____

Writing and Visuals Self-Assessment

Read your writing and make corrections. Answer the questions below to help you check your work.

Writing Assessment

❑ Did I write neatly?

❑ Did I capitalize proper nouns?

❑ Did I use correct end marks?

❑ Did I indent my paragraphs?

❑ Did I check for spelling mistakes?

❑ Did I use complete sentences?

❑ Did I let a friend read my work?

Visual Assessment

❑ Did I complete my project?

❑ Is my project neat?

❑ Did I use labels for my project?

❑ How does my project go with my writing?_____

_____

_____

_____

❑ What will I tell people about my project? _____

_____

_____

_____

Answer Key

Page 19

1. country map
2. city map
3. world map
4. weather map

Page 20

2. West
3. East
4. South
5. North
6.

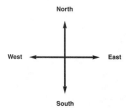

Page 21

2. NE
3. SE
4. SW
5. NW
6.

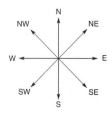

Page 29

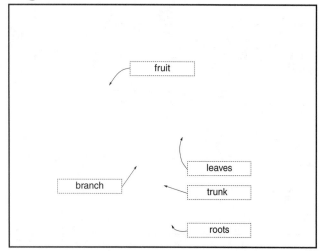

Page 31

Candy Bars

- served in wrappers
- must be chewed

Both

- different flavors
- tastes sweet
- can melt

Ice Cream

- served in cones or dishes
- can be licked
- is frozen

Page 38

1. Five children like lions.
2. Ten children like penguins.
3. Four children like giraffes.
4. Two children like bears.
5. More children like penguins.
6. Six children like bears and giraffes all together.

Page 39

1. Six children like to play sports.
2. Nine children like to watch television.
3. Four children like to play video games.
4. Two children like to do other activities.
5. More children like to watch television.
6. Less children like to play video games.

Page 42

1. Seven children like strawberries.
2. Six children like apples.
3. More children like grapes than bananas.

Page 43

1. Most children like soccer.
2. Two children like to play kickball.
3. One child likes to play tennis.

Answer Key *(cont.)*

Page 45

1. There are eight zebras at the zoo.
2. There are four lions at the zoo.
3. There are twelve monkeys.
4. There are more lions than elephants.
5. There are less zebras than monkeys.

Page 51

1. 4
2. 5
3. 2
4. 6
5. 7
6. 1
7. 8
8. 9
9. 卌
10. ‖
11. 卌 |
12. 卌 ‖‖
13. 卌 卌
14. ‖|
15. 卌 ‖
16. 卌 ‖|

Page 57

1. Memorial Day is on Wednesday.
2. Mother's Day is on the 14th.
3. The last day of school is on Friday, the 19th.
4. The school carnival is on a Saturday.
5. The music performance is on the 2nd.
6. The class party is on a Thursday.

Page 60

1. There are five tables in the classroom.
2. The teacher's desk is along the north wall.
3. The reading circle (or the sink) is north of the classroom library.
4. The reading circle is west of the sink.
5. The hamster cage is closer to the reading circle.

Page 62

1. The school is located on the corner of Maple Street and Pine Avenue.
2. The pizza parlor is north of the post office.
3. The streets that surround the park are Maple, Pine, Aspen, and Elm.
4. The grocery store is closer to the park.

Bibliography

Fiction

Barrett, Judy. *Cloudy with a Chance of Meatballs.* Aladdin Paperbacks, 1982.

Carle, Eric. *The Tiny Seed.* Little Simon, 1998.

Carle, Eric. *The Very Hungry Caterpillar.* Philomel, 1994.

Carter, David A. *Alpha Bugs: A Pop-Up Alphabet.* Little Simon, 1994.

dePaola, Tomie. *Strega Nona.* Aladdin Paperbacks, 1988.

Friedman, Ina. *How My Parents Learned to Eat.* Econo-Clad Books, 1999.

Kirk, David. *Miss Spider's Tea Party.* Scholastic Trade, 1994.

Munsch, Robert. *Angela's Airplane.* Firefly Books, 1988.

O'Neill, Mary. *Hailstones and Halibut Bones.* Doubleday, 1990.

Pallotta, Jerry. *Icky Bug Counting Book.* Econo-Clad Books, 1999.

Sharmat, Mitchell. *Gregory, the Terrible Eater.* Scholastic Trade, 1989.

Westcott, Nadine. *I Know an Old Lady Who Swallowed a Fly.* Econo-Clad Books, 1999.

Related Products from Teacher Created Materials

TCM#167—Beginning Map Skills (Grades 2–4)

TCM#168—Beginning Charts, Graphs, & Diagrams (Grades 2–4)

TCM#2355—How to Use Parts of Speech (Grades 1–3)

TCM#2494—How to Write a Paragraph (Grades 1–3)

TCM#2495—How to Write a Story (Grades 1–3)

TCM#2496—How to Capitalize (Grades 1–3)

TCM#2497—How to Punctuate (Grades 1–3)

TCM#2498—How to Write a Sentence (Grades 1–3)